Daily Discoveries
for August

Thematic Learning Activities for
EVERY DAY

Written by Elizabeth Cole Midgley

Illustrated by Jennette Guymon-King

Teaching & Learning Company

1204 Buchanan St., P.O. Box 10
Carthage, IL 62321-0010

This book belongs to

_____

Cover art by Jennette Guymon-King

Copyright © 2005, Teaching & Learning Company

ISBN No. 1-57310-452-3

Printing No. 987654321

Teaching & Learning Company
1204 Buchanan St., P.O. Box 10
Carthage, IL 62321-0010

Before offering any food to your students, make sure you are aware of any allergies or dietary restrictions your students may have.

At the time of publication every effort was made to insure the accuracy of the information included in this book. However, we cannot guarantee that agencies and organizations mentioned will continue to operate or maintain these current locations.

Table of Contents

Dear Teacher or Parent,

Due to the stimulus of a high-tech world, parents and teachers are often faced with the challenge of how to capture the attention of a child and create an atmosphere of meaningful learning opportunities. Often we search for new ways to meet this challenge and to help young people transfer their knowledge, skills and experiences from one area to another. Subjects taught in isolation can leave a feeling of fragmentation. More and more educators are looking for ways to be able to integrate curriculum so that their students can fully understand how things relate to each other.

The Daily Discoveries series has been developed to that end. The premise behind this series has been, in part, the author's educational philosophy: that anything can be taught and absorbed by others in a meaningful way, depending upon its presentation. In this series, each day has been researched around the history of a specific individual or event and has been developed into a celebration or theme with integrated curriculum areas. In this reality-based approach to learning students draw from their own experience and understanding of things, to a level of processing new information and skills. Each day students can be involved in creating a web or semantic map with what they already know and then add additional information as the day progresses.

The Daily Discoveries is an almanac, of sorts, a 12-book series (one for each month) that presents a thematically based curriculum for grades K-6. The series contains hundreds and hundreds of resources and ideas that can be a natural springboard of learning. These ideas have been used in the classroom and at home and are fun as well as educationally sound. The activities have been endorsed by professors, teachers, parents and, best of all, by children.

The Daily Discoveries series can be used in the following ways for school or home:
- to develop new skills and reinforce previous learning
- to create a sense of fun and celebration every day
- tutoring resources
- enrichment activities that can be used as time allows
- family fun activities

Sincerely,

Elizabeth

Elizabeth Cole Midgley

Shells and Snails Day

August 1

Shells
and
Snails

Shells
and
Snails

Shells
and
Snails

Setting the Stage

• Get a shell collection for a display. Gather travel brochures and posters that illustrate beach areas, places to find lots of shells. Add related literature around the shells. Arrange the shells on sandpaper for a sandy kind of feel.

• Construct a semantic web with all the facts your students know (or would like to know) about shells and snails.

Literary Exploration

Animal Defenses by Malcom Penny
Animals of Sea and Shore by Illa Podendorf
Animals of Seashore by Hidetomo Oda
Animals That Live in Shells by Dean Morris
The Biggest House in the World by Leo Lionni
Clams Can't Sing by James Stevenson
The Crab That Played with the Sea by Rudyard Kipling
Discovering Slugs and Snails by Jennifer Coldrey
Do Not Open by Brinton Turkle
The First Book of Seashells by Betty Cayanna
Hermit Crabs by Kathleen Pohl
A House for Hermit Crab by Eric Carle
The How and Why Wonder Book of Sea Shells by Donald F. Low
How Many Snails?: A Counting Book by Paul Giganti
Is This a House for a Hermit Crab? by Megan McDonald
Junior Science Book of Seashells by Sam and Beryl Epstien
Kermit the Hermit by Bill Peet
On My Beach There Are Many Pebbles by Leo Lionni
Sea Shells of the World by R. Tucker Abbott
The Seashell Song by Susie Jenkin-Pearce
Seashore by Steve Parker
The Seashore Book by E. Boyd Smith
Seashores by Herbert Zim and Lester Ingle
Shells by Alex Arthur
Shells by Jennifer Coldrey
Shells Are Skeletons by Joan Berg Victor
Shells: Where You Can Find Them by
    Elizabeth Clemons
Slugs and Snails by Chris
    Henwood
Slugs and Snails by Colin Walker
Snail in the Woods by Joanne Ryder
Snail, Where Are You? by Tomi Ungerer
Snail's Birthday Problem by Angela McAllister
The Snail's Spell by Joanne Ryder
Snails by Dorothy Childs Hogner
Snails by Silvia Johnson
Snails by Hidetomo Oda
Snails by Herbert Spencer Zim
Snails of Land and Sea by Hilda Simion
Snoopy's Facts and Fun Book About Seashores by Charles M. Shultz
The Story Snail by Anne Rockwell
Treasures in the Sea by Robert McClung
True Book of Pebbles and Shells by Illa Podendort
Why Snails Have Shells by Carolyn Han
Why the Sea Is Salty and Other Questions About Oceans by Anita Ganeri

Shells
and
Snails

Shells
and
Snails

Shells
and
Snails

Language Experience
- Create a Venn diagram depicting the similarities and differences between a shell and a snail.

- Let students brainstorm other words that have the same beginning sounds of *shell* and *snail* (SH and SN). Compare lists by crossing off words that everyone wrote down. Give a prize to the student with the most words. See reproducible on page 10.

Math Experience
- Let students weigh and measure individual and small groups of shells.

- Have students sort, classify and graph shells according to shape, size and texture.

Science/Health Experience
- Today is a great day to learn about the science of snails and their habitat.

- Study different types of shells. Show examples or pictures of some of the more common (scallop, conch, clam, spindle, cowry and sundial). Which ones once housed ocean animals? Leave these at a science nature table with a magnifying glass for further study and observation.

Social Studies Experience

• Are your students aware that in some parts of the world (such as Europe), chocolate-covered snails are considered a food delicacy? Discuss how our culture creates a feeling of acceptance or hesitancy about foods based on what we are accustomed to.

Music/Dramatic Experience

• Encourage your students to come out of their "shells" by playing the Seashell Game! They sit in a circle and pass a seashell around while one person, "it," closes his or her eyes. At a signal, "it" opens his or her eyes and they all say, "Seashell, seashell, who has the seashell?" "It" guesses who has the shell in a closed hand. If "it" is right, that person trades places with whoever had the shell. If not, the game continues and "it" tries again.

Physical/Sensory Experience

• Have a crab relay. Divide students into relay teams to race on all fours like a crab.

• Play a game of Crab Ball! It's just like soccer, only students must play on all fours.

Arts/Crafts Experience

• Let students be inspired by the snail to design their own house-on-the-go! What essentials would they carry with them in their "mobile home"?

Follow-Up/Homework Idea

• Encourage students to begin their own collections of seashell, rocks or whatever!

SOUNDS THE SAME!

Sn

See how many words you can write down that start with SN and SH like <u>sn</u>ail and <u>sh</u>ell!

Sh

Name: _____

Smart Cookies Day

August 2

Setting the Stage

• Decorate a bulletin board with a mock cookie sheet (made from aluminum foil) and giant cookies with a student's name on each. Add the caption: "A Brand-New Batch of Students." See patterns on page 16.

• Leave some cookie crumbs on students' desks to get them excited about the day!

• Wear a chef hat and an apron to "stir" up a little excitement!

• Construct a class semantic map or web with facts the students know (or would like to know) about cookies.

Historical Background

The chocolate chip cookie was invented quite by accident. Out of bakers chocolate, Ruth Wakefield substituted broken pieces of semi-sweetened chocolate in her cookie recipe. After baking the cookies, she was surprised to see that the chocolate pieces did not melt together as she expected. She served them in her Toll House Inn and they were such a big hit they eventually became the most popular cookie in America.

Literary Exploration

The Baby Blue Cat and a Whole Batch of Cookies by Ainslie Pryor
The Chocolate Chip Cookie Contest by Barbara Douglass
Chocolate Chip Cookies by Karen Wagner
Cookie Monster's Story Book by Sesame Street
The Cookie Tree by Jay Williams
Frog and Toad Together by Arnold Lobel
The Good, the Bad and the Two Cookie Kid by Shirley Kelley
If You Give a Mouse a Cookie by Laura Joffe Numeroff
Mike and the Magic Cookies by Jon Buller
Milk and Cookies by Frank Asch
MMM—Cookies!: Simple Subtraction by Nicki Weiss
Mr. Cookie Baker by Monica Wellington
The Oatmeal Cookie Giant by Valiska Gregory
Sam's Cookie by Barbra Lindgren
Who Stole the Cookies? by Judith Moffatt

Language Experience

• For younger students, invite Sesame Street's Cookie Monster to be your temporary mascot. Write skills on cookie shapes. As students say their ABCs, addition facts, etc., they get a "cookie" from Cookie Monster.

Writing Experience

• Supply each student with a paper lunch bag, construction paper, scissors, glue and crayons. Challenge them to design decorator cookie bags. Then have them write the the cookie ingredients and an advertisment on the bags to help their cookies sell!

• Let students write their favorite cookie recipes and compile them into a class cookie cookbook. See patterns on page 17.

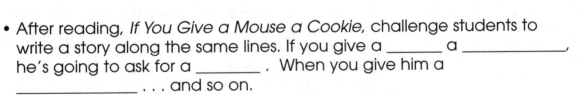

• After reading, *If You Give a Mouse a Cookie,* challenge students to write a story along the same lines. If you give a _____ a _____, he's going to ask for a _____ . When you give him a _____ . . . and so on.

Math Experience

- Students can review measurement (measuring dry or liquid ingredients) as they make cookies.

- Serve homemade, store-bought and slice-and-bake brand cookies for students to taste. Have them create a class graph showing their favorite.

- Have students cut out cookie shapes from construction paper and draw chocolate chips on them (the amount on each cookie will be counted later). Mix everyone's cookies together. Then put a mixture in each student's cookie bag (made earlier). Students count their cookies and sort them. They can use their cookies as math manipulatives but must also write their figures on paper for the teacher to review.

Social Studies Experience

- Encourage responsible thinking and behavior. Discuss the qualities needed to be a "smart cookie" (cooperation, effort, etc.). Let students write the qualities on paper cookies and add them to the bulletin board made earlier. For example: "Smart cookies are hard workers" or "Smart cookies are responsible and finish assignments." Begin an ongoing bulletin board section, "Smart Cookie of the Week." Feature a student each week who demonstrates those behaviors.

Music/Dramatic Experience

- If your students designed cookie bags earlier, let them do presentations to "advertise" to the other students why they should buy their brand of cookies.

Arts/Crafts Experience

• What can students make out of construction paper, yarn, a hole punch, some colored markers and a little creativity? A cookie necklace! Let them be creative with their ideas.

Extension Activities

• Is there a nearby bakery your class can visit? Students will love to watch cookies being made. Have them make observational drawings of the process.

• Serve Cookie Crisp™ cereal for a light treat!

• After reading, *If You Give a Mouse a Cookie* by Laura Joffe Numeroff, make yummy mouse cookies. Give each student two "Snowball" cupcakes (found in grocery stores). Have them put the flat dark side of the cupcakes down. Vanilla wafers can be pushed into the cupcake for "ears," small candies can be "eyes" and "nose" and black licorice laces can be cut for whiskers.

Values Education Experience

• Reinforce what being a "smart cookie" is (responsible choices).

My Favorite Cookie Recipe!

_____
_____
_____
_____
_____

My Favorite Cookie Recipe!

_____
_____
_____
_____

My Favorite Cookie Recipe!

_____
_____
_____
_____

Watermelon Day

August 3

Setting the Stage

• Display student poetry and watermelon art around the caption: "Slice Up Some Poetry!"

• Construct a semantic web with facts your students already know (or would like to know) about watermelons.

Literary Exploration

Great Watermelon Birthday by Vera B. Williams
Leela and the Watermelon by Marilyn Hirsh
One Watermelon Seed by Celia Lottridge
Watermelon Day by Kathi Appelt

Language Experience

• How many new words can your students make from the letters in *watermelon*. See reproducible on page 22.

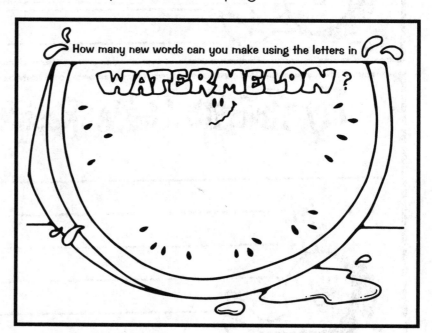

How many new words can you make using the letters in **WATERMELON**?

Writing Experience

• Let students BITE and WRITE! Hand out watermelon slices. Tell them that for every descriptive word they write about watermelon they get to take a bite! Have them use the words to create watermelon poems that can be added to the watermelon sponge paintings they make later.

Math Experience

• Try Watermelon Math! Have students estimate the weight of a watermelon. Weigh it to find out who wins. The one with the closest estimate gets the first slice of watermelon.

• As you slice the watermelon, reinforce the idea of fractions by cutting it in half, then fourths, then eighths and so on.

• Students can estimate the number of seeds inside the watermelon. Then have them count the seeds in their slices and add them together for the actual number.

• Have students count the seeds in their individual slices of watermelon and put the numbers on a class graph. Let students tally all the combined numbers of seeds for a class total.

• Use a small scale to let students measure the weight of their individual slices of watermelon before any of the seeds are taken out. Have them record the data, then add the weight of the slices.

• Let students rinse their watermelon seeds (in a colander) and use them as math manipulatives for "hands on" counting, addition and subtraction practice.

Science/Health Experience
- Study the wonder of a watermelon, actually a vegetable rather than a fruit. Your students might enjoy planting watermelon seeds.

Social Studies Experience
- The watermelon originated in South Africa, but grows more abundantly in China and Turkey than any other place in the world. In some countries, watermelon seeds are roasted and eaten like sunflower seeds.

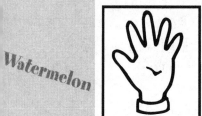

Music/Dramatic Experience
- Borrow and play a sound recording of *Watermelon & Other Stories* by Betty Lehrman from a local library.

Physical/Sensory Experience
- Have a watermelon seed spitting contest! Take students to an out-of-the-way area. See who can spit their seeds the farthest and shortest distances, the fastest and slowest, the highest and even with the most creative spin!

Arts/Crafts Experience

• Cut paper plates in half and have students sponge green paint around the edge. An edge of white goes next and then the final red color. Actual seeds can be glued on for realism!

• Have students make watermelon observational drawings, noting color, thickness and rind imperfections. Let them draw views of the watermelon pieces from different angles around the room.

• Let students dip watermelon rind pieces in paint and make watermelon prints!

Extension Activities

• The day wouldn't be complete without eating a huge slice of juicy, sweet watermelon, just for fun! You might even want to have a watermelon-eating contest!

• Make Watermelon Pops by putting watermelon in a blender, then pouring the liquid into ice cube trays. Stick a craft stick in each cube before freezing them.

Follow-Up/Homework Idea

• Students might suggest their families enjoy watermelon for dessert tonight after dinner.

Watermelon

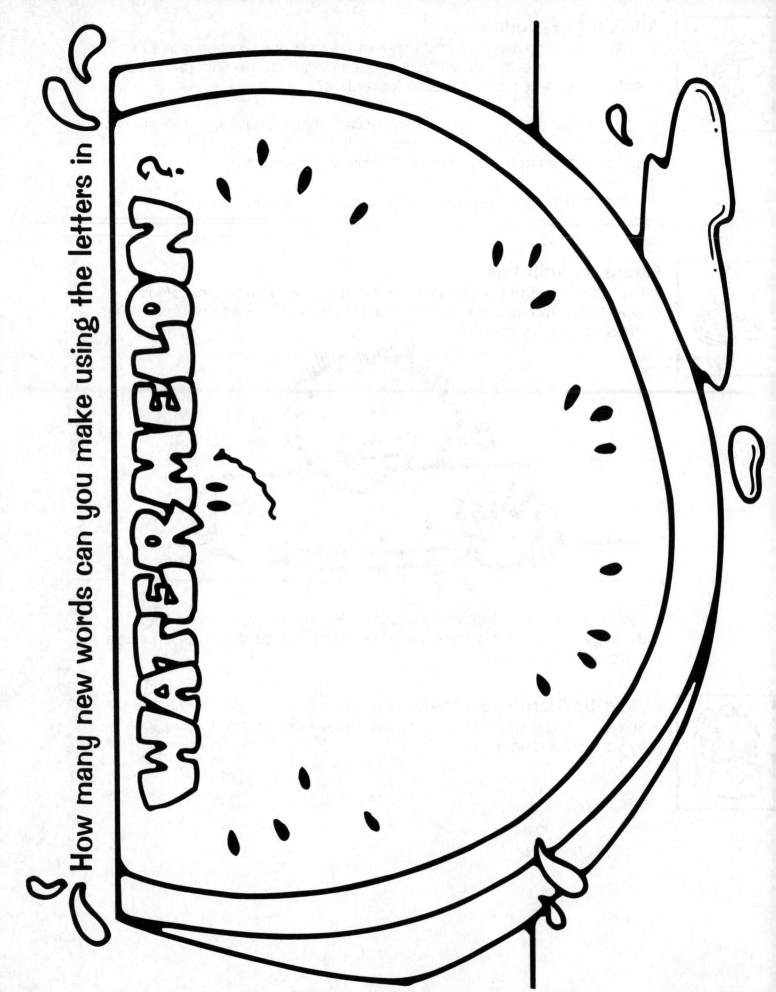

How many new words can you make using the letters in **WATERMELON?**

No Monkeyin' Around Day

August 4

Setting the Stage

- On a bulletin board put a large paper jungle tree. Students can add monkeys swinging from the branches. Later in the day, let students add bananas on the branches. Add the caption: "Keep yourself A-PEELING!" or "Manners or Monkeyin' Around?" See patterns for monkey and bananas on pages 28-30.

- Construct a semantic web with the facts your students know about monkeys, apes, gorillas and chimpanzees. List additional things they want to learn about these furry creatures.

Keep yourself A-PEELING!

Historical Background

This is the time of year when most schools are establishing a new school routine and expectations are set.

Literary Exploration

All Sizes and Shapes of Monkeys and Apes by Richard Armour
Curious George by H.A. Rey
Don't Wake up Mom: Another Five Little Monkeys Jumping on the Bed by Eileen Christelow
A First Look at Monkeys and Apes by Millicent Selsam
Five Little Monkeys by Juliet Kepes
Five Little Monkeys Jumping on the Bed by Eileen Christelow
I Like Monkeys Because... by Peter Hansard
Leopard and the Noisy Monkeys by Giulio Maestro
Little Gorilla by Ruth Bornstein
Miss Nelson Is Back by Harry Allard
Miss Nelson Is Missing by Harry Allard
The Monkey and the Bee by Leland Jacobs
Monkey Business by Nan Bodsworth
Monkey Business by J. Otto Seibold
Monkey in the Middle by Eve Bunting
Monkey Soup by Louis Sachar
Monkeys in the Jungle by Angie Sage
My Monkey? by Dieter Schubert
Not a Little Monkey by Charlotte Zolotow
"Not Me!" Said the Monkey by Colin West
Once There Was a Monkey by E. Dolch
One Little Monkey by Stephanie Calmenson
Two Little Monkeys by Marc Brown
When Monkeys Wore Sombreros by Prieto
Where's Chimpy? by Berniece Rabe
A Wise Monkey Tale by Betsy Maestro

Language Experience

• After revealing your true identity, discuss which kind of teacher your class would want all year, Miss Nelson or Viola Swamp. Also, which a teacher would like to have in her class, students well-behaved or those that act like monkeys. Discuss how similar the behavior in Miss Nelson's class was to that of monkeys. Brainstorm a Venn diagram with the differences and likenesses of monkeys and students.

TLC10452 Copyright © Teaching & Learning Company, Carthage, IL 62321-00

Writing Experience

- Brainstorm class rules together, then have students each write the three most important rules for the classroom. Tally their ideas to help you establish classroom rules. Such as the following:

  1. Please be courteous, respectful and quiet when others are speaking or trying to do their work.

  2. Keep your hands and feet to yourself.

  3. Respect your property and the property of others.

  4. Try to make everyone your friend.

- Write silly rules! Such as: "Rules for Washing Your Face" or "Rules for Eating an Ice Cream Bar." See reproducible on page 31.

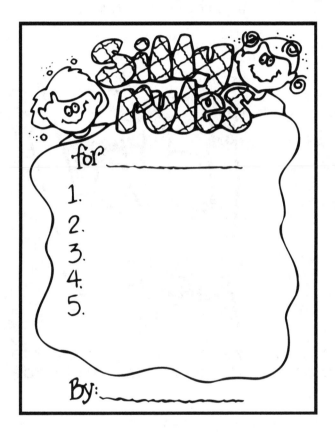

Science/Health Experience

- Learn about monkeys, apes, gorillas and chimpanzees and their habitats.

Social Studies Experience

- Brainstorm manners or monkeyin' around situations. Write them on banana shapes and attach them to the bulletin board.

- Discuss the importance of everyone feeling safe and appreciated with an equal opportunity to learn. Allow 30 seconds of noise-making chaos to let students observe how difficult it would be to learn in such an environment.

Physical/Sensory Experience

- Play on the "monkey" bars in your school playground!

- Play Monkey See, Monkey Do, letting students take turns pantomiming actions for other students to mimic.

- Have Monkey Relays! Divide the class into relay teams. Students must grab their ankles or run on all fours to a designated area and back.

Arts/Crafts Experience

- Have students write down and illustrate your new classroom rules.

- Let students use brown pipe cleaners to shape monkeys.

Extension Activities

• Make chocolate frozen bananas! Buy chocolate syrup which hardens or melt chocolate chips. Dip a banana-on-a-stick into the chocolate mixture and roll in nuts. Then freeze them for a yummy snack.

• Find a game of, Barrel of Monkeys. Let students play it for a great exercise in physical dexterity.

• Blend bananas and vanilla ice cream to make a "monkey malt."

Follow-Up/Homework Idea

• Encourage students to continue their good manners and avoid acting like "monkeys" both at school and home.

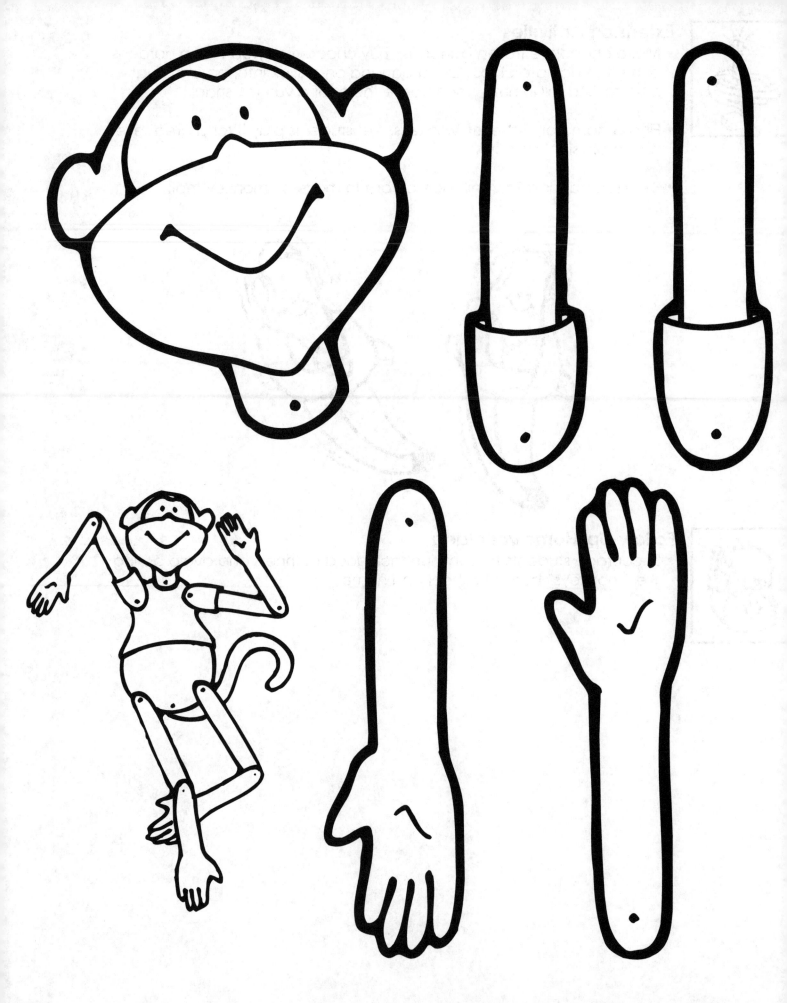

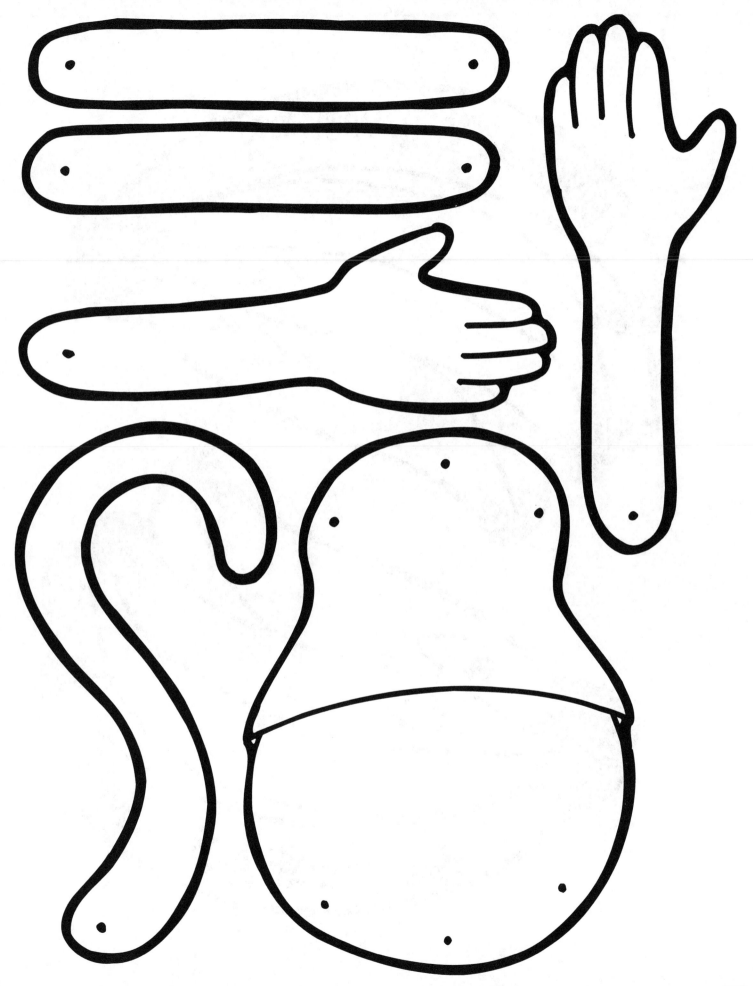

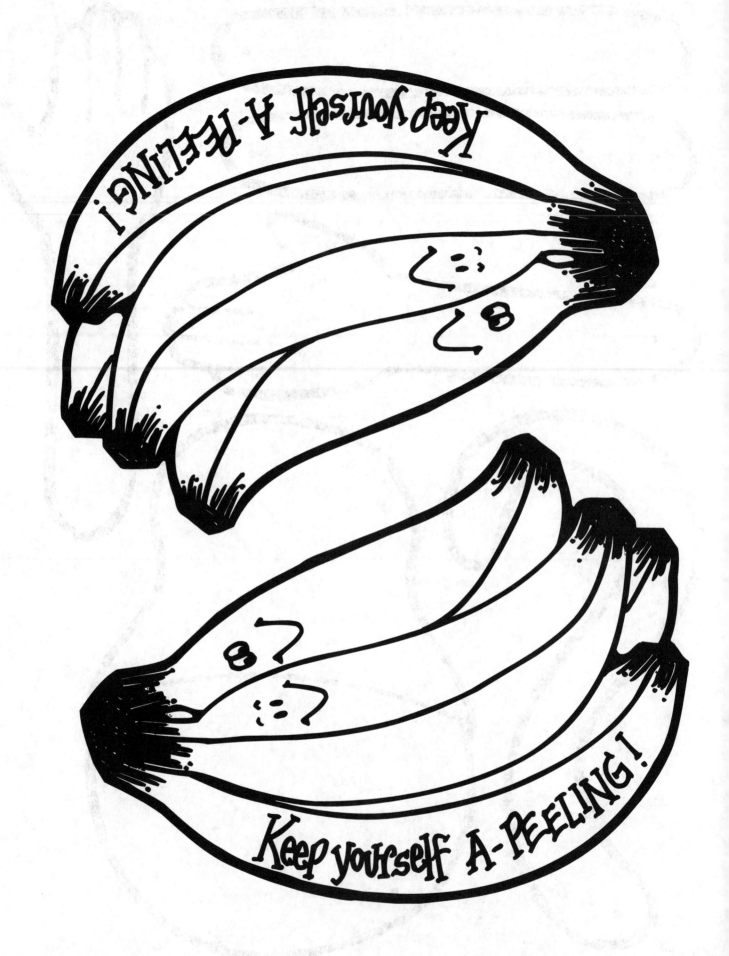

Silly rules

for _____

1.
2.
3.
4.
5.

By: _____

Friendship Day

August 5
(varies)

Setting the Stage

- Display pictures of friends (enjoying being together, helping each other, solving problems together) around related literature.

- Construct a semantic web with the things your students think of when you say the word *friend*.

Literary Exploration
329th Friend by Marjorie Weinman Sharmat
Are You My Friend? by Dick Dudley
Ben Finds a Friend by Ann Marie Chapouton
Best Friends by Miriam Cohen
Best Friends by Steven Kellogg
Best Friends by Jocelyn Stevenson
Bridge to Terabithia by Katherine Paterson
But Names Will Never Hurt Me by Bernard Waber
Clancy's Coat by Eve Bunting
The Doorbell Rang by Pat Hutchins
Even If I Did Something Awful? by Barbara Shook Hazen
The Friend by John Burningham
A Friend Is Someone Who Likes You by Joan Anglund
Friends by Helme Heine
Friends! Friends! Friends! by Ruth Jaynes
Frog and Toad Are Friends by Arnold Lobel
Grandfather's Journey by Allen Say
How I Found a Friend by Irina Hale
I Have a Friend by Keiko Narhashi
I Need a Friend by Sherry Kafka
Ira Says Goodbye by Bernard Waber
Just My Friend and Me by Mercer Mayer
Let's Be Enemies by Janice Udry
Let's Be Friends Again by Hans Wilhelm
Loop the Loop by Barbara Dugan

Literary Exploration continued

Making Friends by Margaret Mahy
Making Friends by Eleanor Schick
My Best Friend by Pat Hutchins
My Friend Jacob by Lucille Clifton
My Friend Leslie by Maxine B. Rosenberg
The New Friend by Charlotte Zolotow
Rosie and Michael by Judith Viorst
The Secret Garden by Frances Hodgson Burnett
That's What a Friend Is by P.K. Halinan
Thy Friend, Obadiah by Brinton Turkle
Two Good Friends by Judy Delton
We Are Best Friends by Aliki
A Weekend with Wendell by Kevin Henkes
We're Very Good Friends, My Brother and I by P.K. Halinan
Where Is My Friend? by Betsy Maestro
The Whipping Boy by Sid Fleishman
Who Will Be My Friend? by Syd Hoff
Will I Have a Friend? by Miriam Cohen
Will You Be My Friend? by Irmtraut Korth-Sander

Language Experience

• Let students brainstorm as many words as they can that rhyme with the word *friend* or that begin with the "fr" sound.

• Let students list their friends' names. Then have them alphabetize the names. You may use the reproducible on page 38 for this activity.

Writing Experience

- Let students have fun writing a classified ad (found in newspapers) for a new friend. They may include the qualities they hope to find in a friend and what they can offer in return (companionship, loyalty, etc.). When everyone's ad has been received, post them for everyone to read. Encourage students to answer the ads. See reproducible on page 38.

Friendship

- Let students write about one of these ideas:

  A friend is for . . .
  You can tell someone likes you by . . .
  My best friends and I . . .

Math Experience

- Reinforce the idea that friends help each other. Divide students into pairs to help each other with mental math facts (addition, subtraction or multiplication).

Friendship

Science/Health Experience

- Explain that having friends is important to our growth, health and emotional development. Having friends makes us feel good inside. Students need to know that it's not healthy to be alone all the time. We need to be a help and benefit to one another.

34

TLC10452 Copyright © Teaching & Learning Company, Carthage, IL 62321-001

Social Studies Experience

- Discuss the qualities of a friend. Let students see you model kindness, courtesy, respect and thoughtfulness.

- Discuss how we can have a variety of friendships: within our families, in our neighborhoods and school, with older and younger friends and animal friends. We can even be our own best friend! Discuss how friends can be like us or different than us.

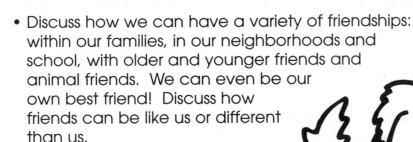

Music/Dramatic Experience

- Let students role-play various situations that model getting along with others and problem solving.

Physical/Sensory Experience

- Involve students in cooperative physical exercises or activities where they have to rely on one another and cooperate for the benefit of their team: potato or gunny sack races, three-legged relay races or water balloon toss.

- Play Friendship Bingo! Write friends names in the Bingo squares (the more varied the names, the better their chances of winning). Play according to Bingo rules. See cards on page 39.

Arts/Crafts Experience

• Create a Friendship Quilt! Give each student a piece of white muslin or a square of an old sheet (make sure all squares are the same size) and a permanent or fabric marker. Students draw pictures and write their names on their squares. Enlist the help of a parent to sew the pieces together into a quilt. You may prefer to glue paper squares together for a paper quilt. Display your Friendship Quilt in the room so students can see the results of their cooperative effort.

• Show students how to make a chain of paper dolls. Draw a different friend's face on each paper doll and write an attribute that the person has or that you appreciate.

• Let students draw self-portraits (from head to toe). Have them label their pictures, *I am a Good Friend*. They can draw a line from a body part to a caption that tells what they do as a friend.
Example: head—"I HEAD for help when needed;" nose—"I'm a friend who NOSE how to be trustworthy"; eyes—"I LOOK for ways to show kindness"; shoulders—"I can be a SHOULDER to lean on"; hands—"I can lend a HAND"; hear—"I show that I care." See reproducible on page 40.

TLC10452 Copyright © Teaching & Learning Company, Carthage, IL 62321-001

Extension Activities

• Host a Friendship Scavenger Hunt Party! Students fold a sheet of paper in fourths then eighths. They unfold the paper and draw a picture in each section of what they like to do (read, bike, play with their pet, roller-blade). When all the sections are filled in, students try to find friends in the room who also like to do those things to autograph the appropriate sections. Serve punch ("friends frappe") and cookies. Let students "mingle" with their friends, sharing their common interests.

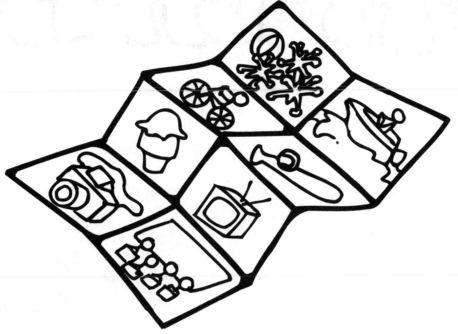

Values Education Experience

• Discuss the value of having and maintaining friendships throughout our lives.

Follow-Up/Homework Idea

• Encourage each student to make at least one more new friend by the end of the day and to be a better friend to family members.

Friends

Name: _____

I am a good friend!

Name: _____

Busy Bee Day

August 6

Setting the Stage

• Display student work alongside paper bees with the caption: "BEE-utiful Work!" "We've Been Busy as Little BEES!" or "_____ (fill in grade) is un-BEE-lievably fun!" See patterns for students to color on page 45.

• Display a container of honey and products made from beeswax such as candles, ointments and polishes.

Historical Background

Before sugar was taken from sugarcane, honey was the sweetener people used.

Literary Exploration

The Bee by Lisa Campbell Ernst
Bee by David Hawcock
The Bee: Friend of the Flowers by Paul Starosta
A Beekeeper's Year by Sylvia Johnson
The Bee Tree by Patricia Pollacco
Bees and Beelines by Judy Hawes
"Buzz," Said the Bee by Wendy Lewison
Harry's Bee by Peter Campbell
The Rose in My Garden by Arnold Lobel
Watch Honeybees with Me by Judy Hawes

Language Experience

• Have a spelling BEE! Encourage students to study their spelling words, then have a Group Spelling Bee to encourage group effort. When a group is given a word, they can discuss it together for about 15 seconds, then choose one person to spell the word.

Writing Experience

• Students can write their feelings with a story starter such as "I like my class BEE-cause . . . ." Let them write on the blank side of a bee pattern from page 45.

42

Science/Health Experience

- Today is a great day to begin a science unit on bees! Do your students know that this interesting insect has five eyes (two on the sides and three in the middle of his forehead) and is the only insect that can produce food that is eaten by people? Of the more than 20,000 different species of bees, only the honeybee makes honey, mixing enzymes inside their bodies with nectar they find in flowers.

- If you have access to a real honeycomb, show students what is on the inside. A honeycomb has six-sided wax cells where honey is stored.

- Review safety precautions to take around bees (especially in case of bee allergies).

- Let students diagram and identify the parts of a bee: the head with its eyes, antennae and tongue; the thorax with forewings and legs and the abdomen with its pollen basket and stinger.

Music/Dramatic Experience

- Borrow from a local library a sound recording of "The Flight of the Bumblebee."

Physical/Sensory Experience
• Younger students will enjoy a chance to buzz around like bees!

Arts/Crafts Experience
• Let students make bumblebees with white tissue paper or waxed paper wings.

Extension Activities
• Invite a local beekeeper to come and visit your class and talk about working with bees.

• Serve honey on crackers or Honeycomb™ cereal for a fun treat!

• Let students shape Rice Krispy™ Treats into a beehive (oval) shape for a "honey" of a snack!

Follow-Up/Homework Idea
• Encourage students to continue to be as busy as bees in and out of school.

44

Jurassic Spark Day

August 7

Setting the Stage

- Children have a natural fascination for dinosaurs. Capitalize on this interest with a display of toy and plastic dinosaurs, as well as pictures around related literature. Create dinosaur-looking footprints leading into your classroom. See footprint pattern on page 52.

- Construct a semantic web around what your students already know about dinosaurs, then list questions for what they would like to learn about them.

Historical Background

Today marks the birthday of Louis B. Leakey, an anthropologist and paleontologist (someone who goes on archaeological digs) who was born on this day in 1903.

Literary Exploration

Baby Dinosaurs by Helen Sattler
Bones, Bones, Dinosaur Bones by Byron Barton
Daniel's Dinosaurs by Mary Carmine
Danny and the Dinosaurs by Syd Hoff
Digging up Dinosaurs by Aliki
Digging up Tyrannosaurus Rex by Horner and Gorman
Dinosaur Bob and His Adventures with Family Lazardo by William Joyce
Dinosaur Dan by Randall Reinstedt
Dinosaur Dream by Dennis Nolan
Dinosaur Riddles by Joseph Heck
Dinosaurs by Mary Lou Clark
Dinosaurs by Eunice Holsaert
Dinosaurs by Lee Bennett Hopkins
Dinosaurs by David Lambert
Dinosaurs and All That Rubbish by Michael Foreman
Dinosaurs Are Different by Aliki
Dinosaurs, Dinosaurs by Byron Barton
Dinosaur's Housewarming Party by Norma Klein
Dinosaur Time by Peggy Parish
The Dinosaur Who Lived in My Backyard by B. G. Hennessy
Dinotopia: A Land Apart from Time by James Gurney
Enormous Egg by Oliver Butterworth
A Family of Dinosaurs by Mary O'Neill
A First Look at Dinosaurs by Joyce Hunt
Fossils Tell of Long Ago by Aliki
Giant Dinosaurs by Erna Rowe
How I Captured a Dinosaur by Henry Schwartz
The Largest Dinosaurs by Seymour Simon
Learning About Dinosaurs by Dougal Dixon
The Little Dinosaur and the Big Carnival by Sara James
Maia: A Dinosaur Grows Up by John R. Horner
My Visit to the Dinosaurs by Aliki
New Questions & Answers About Dinosaurs by Seymour Simon
Prehistoric Monsters Do the Strangest Things by Leonora and Arthur
  Hornblow
Prehistoric Pinkerton by Steven Kellogg
Prehistoric Reptiles by Dougal Dixon
Quiet on Account of Dinosaur by Jane Thayer
The Secret Dinosaur by Marilyn Hirsh
The Smallest Dinosaurs by Seymour Simon
Time Train by Paul Fleishman
The Tyrannosaurus Game by Steven Kroll
Tyrannosaurus Was a Beast by Jack Prelutsky
Wackysaurus Dinosaur Jokes by Louis Phillips
What Ever Happened to the Dinosaurs? by Bernard Most
What Happened to Patrick's Dinosaurs? by Carol Carrick
What Happened to the Dinosaurs? by Franklyn M. Branley
The Wonderful Egg by Dahlov Ipcar

Jurassic Spark

Jurassic Spark

Jurassic Spark

Language Experience

- Let students brainstorm names of different kinds of dinosaurs, (Brachiosaurus, Triceratops, Stegosaurus, Tyrannosaurus) then put the names in alphabetical order.

Writing Experience

- Let students write about why they think dinosaurs became extinct. See reproducible on page 53.

I think dinosaurs are extinct because...

Name: _____

Math Experience

- Let your students try to imagine how big some of the largest dinosaurs were by marking out the dimensions on the playground. Ankylosaurus was estimated to be 15 feet; Stegosaurus and Triceratops measured about 25 feet; Tyrannosaurus was estimated at 50 feet; Diplodocus and Apatosaurus ran about 85 feet and Ultrasaurus was 100 feet or more!

Science/Health Experience

- Today is the perfect opportunity to begin a unit on dinosaurs!

Social Studies Experience

• With a world atlas, locate where dinosaurs have been found. (Triceratops, Trachodon, Allosaurus and Diplodocus have been found in North America; Antarctosaurus and Saltasaurus have been located in South America; Apatosaurus and Stegosaurus in Europe; Oviraptor, Ultrasaurus and Protoceratops in Asia and Brachiosaurus and Iguanodon in Africa.)

Music/Dramatic Experience

• Check out "Dinosaur Rock" or "Walk the Dinosaur" (sound recordings) from your local library.

• Let interested students perform stand-up comic routines using jokes in *Colossal Fossils: Dinosaur Riddles* compiled by Charles Kelle or *Tyrannosaurus Wrecks: A Book of Dinosaur Riddles* written by Noelle Sterne.

Physical/Sensory Experience

• Don the Dinosaur Binoculars and Cave-Man Suit (to be made later in the Arts/Crafts Experience) to go on a class Dinosaur Hunt!

• Let students see how fossils are made by letting them press small objects (paper clips or small shells) into flattened mounds of clay. Explain that when a dinosaur stepped into soft rock or mud, it left an impression which hardened into a fossil over the years.

• Play a dinosaur version of Musical Chairs with this game of Extinction. Students can decide what kind of dinosaurs they are before playing, then see which is the last to become extinct!

• Let each student create an "edible Stegosaurus!" Give each a bend-able straw, pumpkin seeds, a hand-ful of toothpicks and large marsh-mallows. Students thread the large marshmallows along the straw (dinosaur spine) to create the base of the body. Dinosaur legs and feet can be made by skewering addi-tional marshmallows onto toothpicks. Pumpkin seeds on top of the Stegosaurus can be protective armored plates.

Arts/Crafts Experience

- Dinosaur Binoculars can be made by painting two toilet paper tubes gray or coloring the pattern on page 54, covering the tubes with it and gluing them together. Punch holes for a string that can be hung loosely around a student's neck.

- A Cave-Man Suit can be made by cutting a large brown grocery bag to go around one shoulder (Fred Flintstone-style). Have students paint black and dark brown splotches on the bags to resemble an animal skin.

- Let your fast finishers work on a mural of cave-man paintings.

- Other students can shape dinosaurs from aluminum foil.

- Students will enjoy creating a dinosaur shadow box from a shoe box, small plastic greenery and toy dinosaurs.

Extension Activities

- Serve a prehistoric treat of gummy dinosaurs or Dinosaur Grahams™ (graham crackers) in triangular cups (white envelope corners cut at an angle). The container will look like a dinosaur tooth!

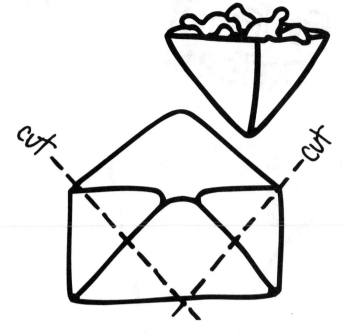

- If your students get thirsty, let them sip Prehistoric Punch. Before class, freeze small plastic dinosaurs in water in an ice cube tray. When they are completely frozen, place the cubes in glasses of water. Tell your students that the Ice Age is over and the dinosaurs may be thawed. They need to be on the lookout for possible dinosaur sightings! If you decide not to have punch, make the Ice Age dinosaurs for a game of seeing who can "defrost" their dinosaur the fastest!

- Serve Dinosaur Eggs (hard-boiled eggs), Sleeping Brontosaurus' (croissants) and Dinosaur Stew!

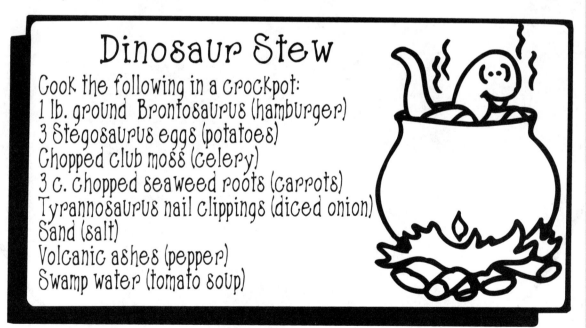

Dinosaur Stew

Cook the following in a crockpot:
1 lb. ground Brontosaurus (hamburger)
3 Stegosaurus eggs (potatoes)
Chopped club moss (celery)
3 c. chopped seaweed roots (carrots)
Tyrannosaurus nail clippings (diced onion)
Sand (salt)
Volcanic ashes (pepper)
Swamp water (tomato soup)

- If you live near a dinosaur exhibit or a museum that specializes in prehistoric fossils, why not take your students on a class field trip?

FOOTPRINT PATTERN

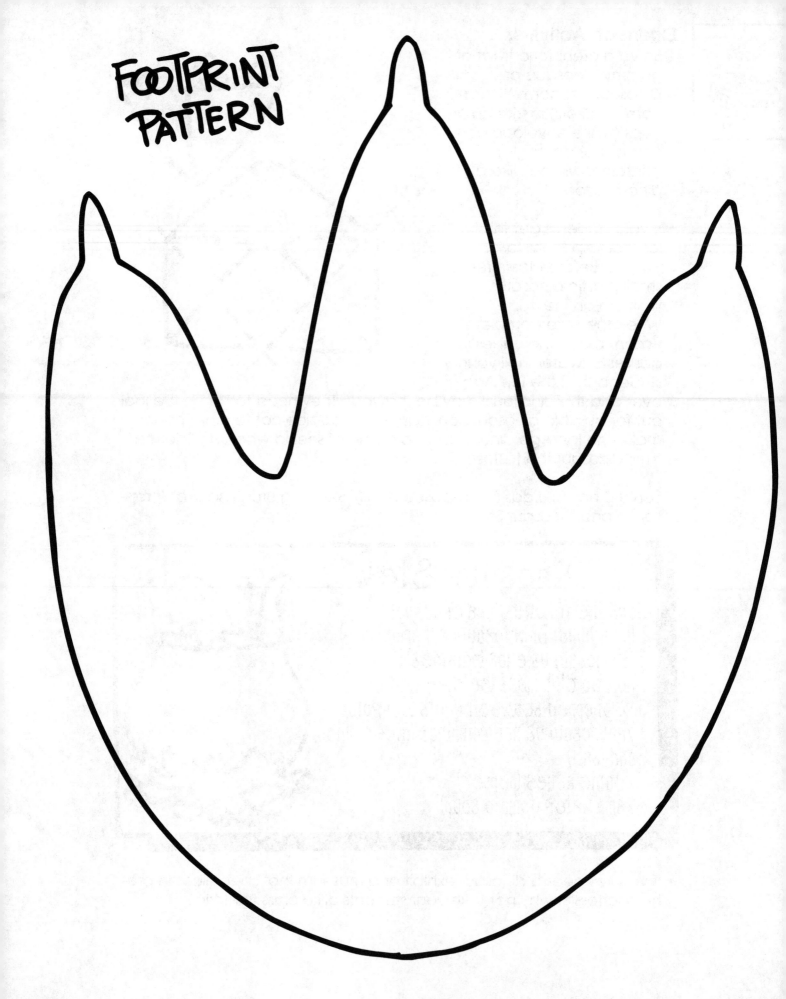

I think dinosaurs are extinct because...

Name: _____

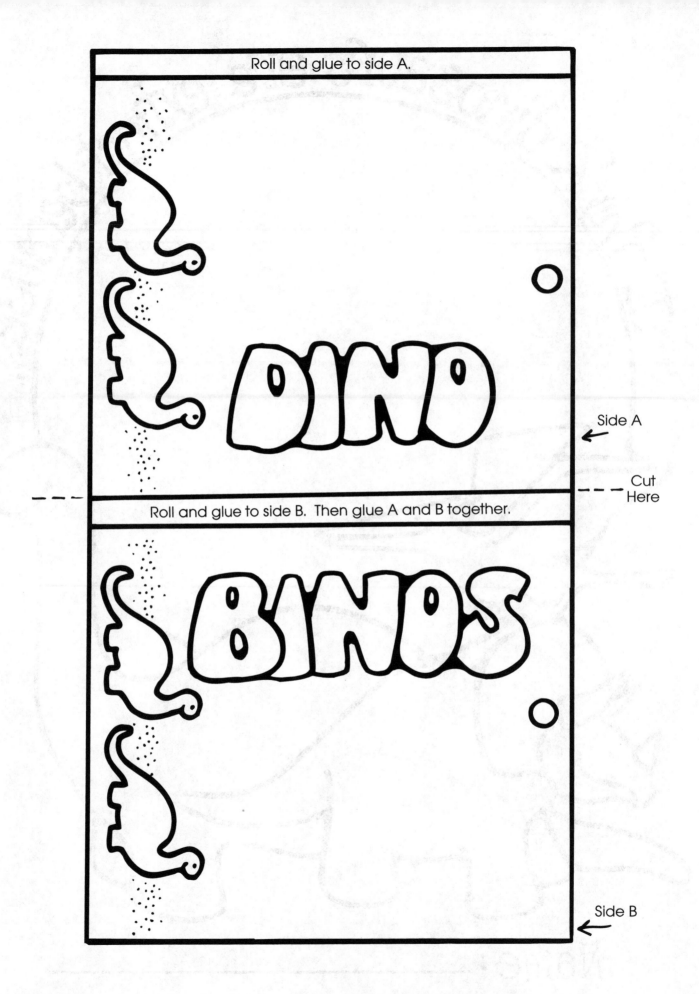

Roll and glue to side A.

DINO

Side A

Cut Here

Roll and glue to side B. Then glue A and B together.

BINOS

Side B

This Is Your Life Day

August 8

Setting the Stage

• Ask students to bring in baby pictures and current pictures of themselves. Display these on a bulletin board. Number them and add the caption: "Guess Who's Growing Up?"

• Show your students pictures of yourself over the years so they can see the progression from infant to toddler to child to adult.

• Construct a semantic web with words your students think of when you say the word *life*.

Literary Exploration

Look How a Baby Grows by Giovanna Mantegazza
Mostly Michael by Robert Kimmel Smith
My Book About Me by Dr. Suess

Language Experience

• Have students brainstorm words that rhyme with *life*.

This Is
Your Life

This Is
Your Life

This Is
Your Life

Writing Experience

- Let students look at their baby pictures and write what they might have been thinking at the time. They can write their creative ideas in speech bubbles next to the pictures on the bulletin board.

- Challenge students to make ME Books! Have them begin self-portraits (from head to toe). The face can be drawn or a round piece of foil can be used for a mirrored effect. Staple the pages together and fill them with personal information. See reproducibles on pages 59-62.

- Let students write about their first memories.

- Let students write from one of these story starters:

    If I were older, I would . . .
    When I was little . . .
    I know how to . . .
    When my parents were my age, they . . .
    I finally know . . .
    I finally can . . .
    The craziest thing I've ever done was when . . .
    The worst thing that could happen to me is . . .
    The bravest thing I've ever done is . . .
    I think the most special day in my life so far was . . .

TLC10452 Copyright © Teaching & Learning Company, Carthage, IL 62321-00

Science/Health Experience

• Begin a health unit on growing up.

UP and UP!

Social Studies Experience

• Have students make time lines of their lives depicting some significant events, such as: birth, first steps, starting school and so on.

Music/Dramatic Experience

• Let students play charades acting out what they hope to do someday as their classmates try to guess.

Physical/Sensory Experience

- Let students try to match the baby pictures on the bulletin board with the current pictures of their classmates.

- Show students how much they have changed (including their dietary habits) by letting them try eating baby food again! Divide them into pairs. Give each student a small paper plate, a plastic spoon and a blob of baby food. One student tries to feed the other. After a few minutes, they trade roles.

Arts/Crafts Experience

- Have students fold a sheet of paper into thirds. On the first section they write *Past,* on the middle section, *Present* and on the last section, *Future.* Let them illustrate events in their lives in the correct sections.

Extension Activities

- Invite a parent with children of varying ages to talk to your class about each stage of life.

Values Education Experience

- This is a great opportunity to talk about the precious gift of life and its value.

Follow-Up/Homework Idea

- Encourage students to begin writing an ongoing journal or autobiography at home.

MY BOOK ABOUT ME

BY: _____

THIS IS ME...
from HEAD

to TOE!

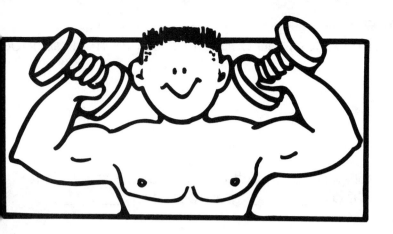

Body Beautiful Day

August 9

Setting the Stage

- Display a plastic model and pictures of the human body around related literature.

- Construct a semantic web with facts your students already know about the human body. Ask your students to list additional things that they would like to find out about the body.

Literary Exploration

At the Doctor by A. Grunsell
Blood and Guts by Linda Allison
Dinosaurs Alive and Well: A Guide to Good Health by Laurie and Marc Brown
A Drop of Blood by Paul Showers
Going to the Doctor by Fred Rogers
How and Why: A Kid's Book About the Body by C. O'Neill
How Many Teeth? by Paul Showers
Human Body by L. Cohen
The Human Body and How It Works by Angela Royston
The Human Body by Joanna Cole
The Human Body by Jonathan Miller
Junior Body Machine by Christiaan Barnard
Look Inside Your Body by Gina Ingoglia
A New True Book About Health by K. Jacobsen
The Magic School Bus Inside the Human Body by Joanna Cole
Ouch! A Book About Cuts, Scratches, and Scrapes by Melvin Berger
Vitamins: What They Are, What They Do by Judith Seixas
What's Inside? My Body by Dorling Kindersley
Why Do Our Bodies Stop Growing? by Phillip Whitfield
Why I Blink and Other Questions About My Body by Brigid Avison
You Can't Make a Move Without Your Muscles by Paul Showers
Your Teeth by J. Iveson

Language Experience

• Have students brainstorm parts of the body, then put them in alphabetical order.

Writing Experience

• Let students write silly stories by filling in the blanks of this story starter, then elaborating on it: "If a _____ grew out of my _____ . . ."

Math Experience

• Let students practice their measuring skills by measuring from one area of their bodies to another: from the fingertip to elbow, from toes to heel, from hip to knee and so on. Let them measure using a centimeter ruler and/or inch ruler or a measuring tape.

Science/Health Experience

- Today is the perfect opportunity to begin a health and science unit on the human body.

- Have students cut out a paper doll chain. As they learn about a body part function, they can illustrate where it is on one of the paper dolls and write a fascinating fact about that body part on the doll. Soon they'll have a whole chain of interesting information.

- Divide older students into cooperative groups to research body systems (respiratory, endocrine, circulatory, muscular, skeletal and so on). Have them share their findings with the rest of the class. See reproducible on page 68.

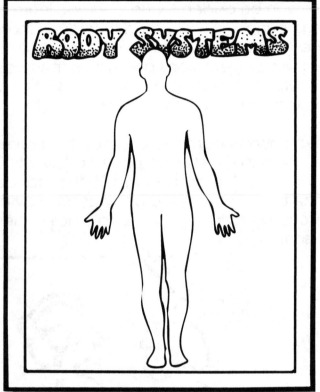

Music/Dramatic Experience

- Give students an opportunity to advertise healthy living! Divide the class into cooperative groups. Let them decide what aspect they want to cover (nutrition, safety, dental care, exercise, rest, hygiene). Encourage them to be creative as they make posters, write jingles or perform television commercials.

Physical/Sensory Experience

• Play this crazy mixed-up game! Choose a student to give a signal and movement for the others to follow. They touch the body parts as they are mentioned, but not necessarily modeled. The first two body parts are the same, but the third is a surprise. Example: The leader says, "Eye, eye, nose," but touches his eyes, then his elbow. Everyone has to pay attention or they will do the wrong action!

Arts/Crafts Experience

• Trace loosely around students' bodies on butcher paper. Let them cut out the outline and trace another likeness on a second sheet. Staple the two figures together on one side and let students draw features. Yarn can be added for hair. As you learn about internal parts (heart, lungs, bones), students can then draw them in the correct places. When the body parts have all been drawn, they can stuff the two outlines with paper scraps and staple them together for a three-dimensional figure. Let them seat their bodies at their desks to surprise parents at an Open House or Back-to-School Night.

• Have each student find a picture of a human body in a magazine, cut it in half and give half to another student. They must try to draw the other half of the body to match the magazine half. Discuss symmetry in the body. Or make a body collage by cutting body parts from vairous magazine pictures and placing them together to make a new person!

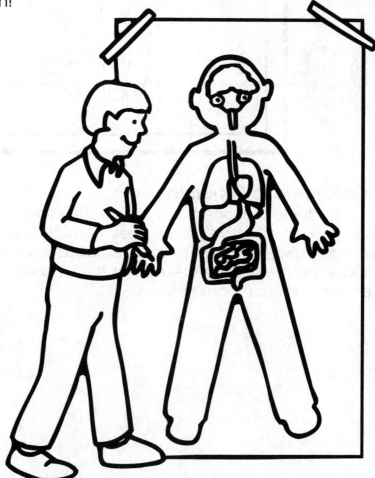

Values Education Experience
- Discuss the importance of appreciating and maintaining a healthy body.

Follow-Up/Homework Idea
- Encourage students to be good examples to their families of keeping their bodies in tip-top shape!

BODY SYSTEMS

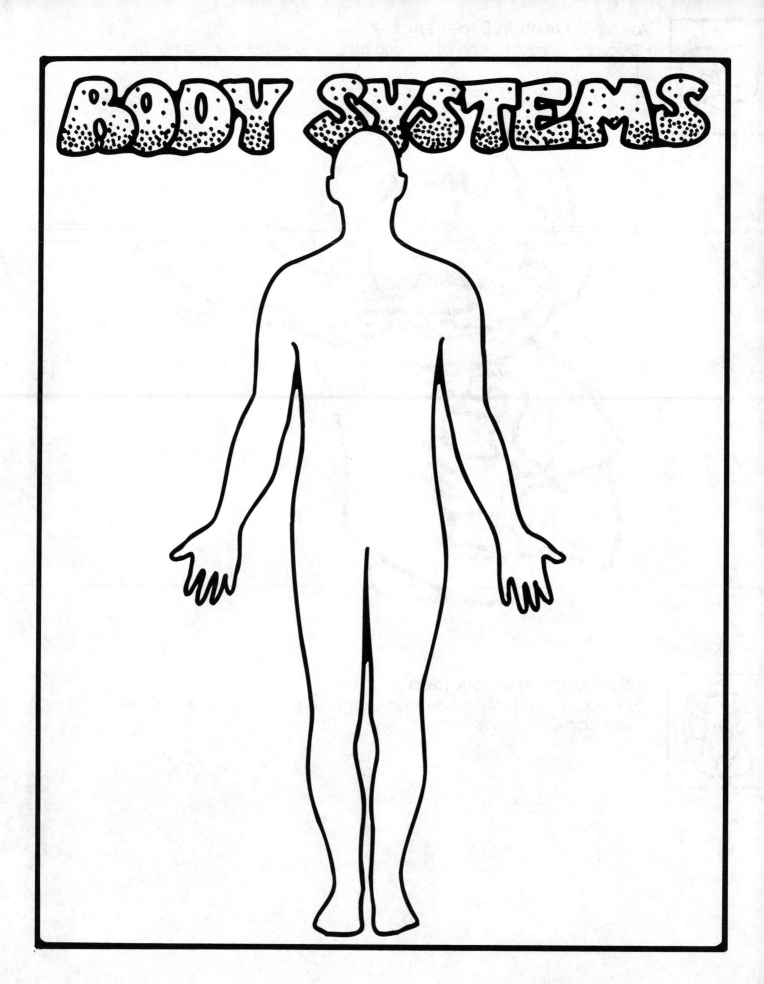

Goin' on a Bear Hunt Day

August 10

Setting the Stage

• Display student handwriting samples with a stuffed bear toy or picture of a bear and the caption: "Our BEARY Best Handwriting!"

• Leave authentic-looking bear tracks leading into your room and across the front board to get your students excited about the day. See patterns on pages 73-74.

• Construct a semantic web with facts your students already know (or want to know) about bears.

Literary Exploration

Alaska's Three Bears by Shelly Gill
Are You There, Bear? by Ron Maris
Bearman by Laurence Pringle
Bear's in the Forest by Karen Wallace
The Bear Who Had No Place to Go by James Stevenson
The Berenstain Bears (series) by Stan Berenstain
Bicycle Bear by Michaela Muntean
Big Bad Bruce by Bill Peet
The Biggest Bear by Lynd Ward
Blackboard Bear by Martha Alexander
Blueberries for Sal by Robert McCloskey
Brown Bear, Brown Bear, What Do You See? by Bill Martin
Can't You Sleep Little Bear? by Martin Waddell
Deep in the Forest by Brinton Turkle
Every Autumn Comes the Bear by Jim Arnosky
Eyewitness Juniors: Amazing Bears by Theresa Greenaway
Golden Bear by Ruth Young
Good Morning, Granny Rose by Warren Ludwig
Grizzwold by Syd Hoff
Happy Birthday, Moon by Frank Asch
Helen the Hungry Bear by Marilyn MacGregor
How Do Bears Sleep? by E. J. Bird
The Lazy Bear by Michael Wildsmith
The Little Mouse, the Red Ripe Strawberry and the Big Hungry Bear by
    Don and Audrey Wood

*Bear
Hunt*

*Bear
Hunt*

*Bear
Hunt*

Literary Exploration continued

The Smartest Bear and His Brother Oliver by Alice Bach
Two Bear Cubs by Ann Jonas
We're Goin' on a Bear Hunt by Michael Rosen
Where's the Bear? by Byron Barton

Language Experience

• Review homonyms (words like *bear* and *bare*) with students.

Writing Experience

• Let students write about how they feel when they are "Being Their BEARY Best Self!"

• You may prefer to have them write about their "Most Un-BEAR-able Day!" See reproducible on page 75.

Math Experience

- Most zoos do not want you to feed the bears, but this is a bear you can feed. Copy the pattern on page 76. Cut out the mouth and glue the face to an empty tissue box. Copy the berries on page 77 for each student. Have students write a number between 1-20 on each one, then cut them out. Pose some mathematical problems (such as 5 + 8 or 25 - 5). Those with the answer on a strawberry get to feed the bear!

Science/Health Experience

- Today is a perfect day to learn about bears and their habitat.

- Review camping safety in areas where there might be bears nearby.

Bear Hunt

Social Studies Experience

• Locate on a map parts of the country where bears are likely to live.

Music/Dramatic Experience

• Sing some traditional favorites such as "The Bear Went over the Mountain" and "Goin' on a Bear Hunt!"

Physical/Sensory Experience

• A bear places its whole foot down when it walks (rather than walking on the ball of the foot like a human). Let students try walking flat-footed like a bear.

Arts/Crafts Experience

• Challenge students to draw a grizzly bear, then glue brown tissue paper squares all over it. Use the tip of a pencil eraser to put the pieces in place.

• Try making a bear from fake fur found in craft stores.

Extension Activities

• Visit a local zoo to check out the bears!

• Serve Bear Claws (pastries) for a treat!

Follow-Up/Homework Idea

• Encourage students to go on a nature walk with their families, then make a collage with items they find.

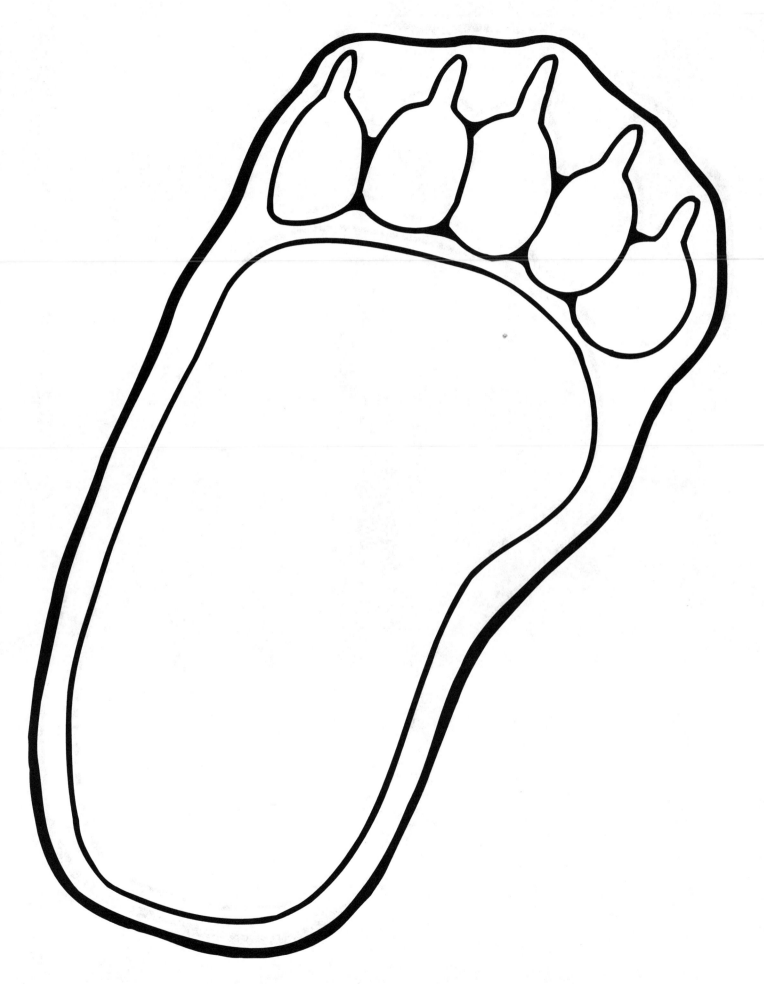

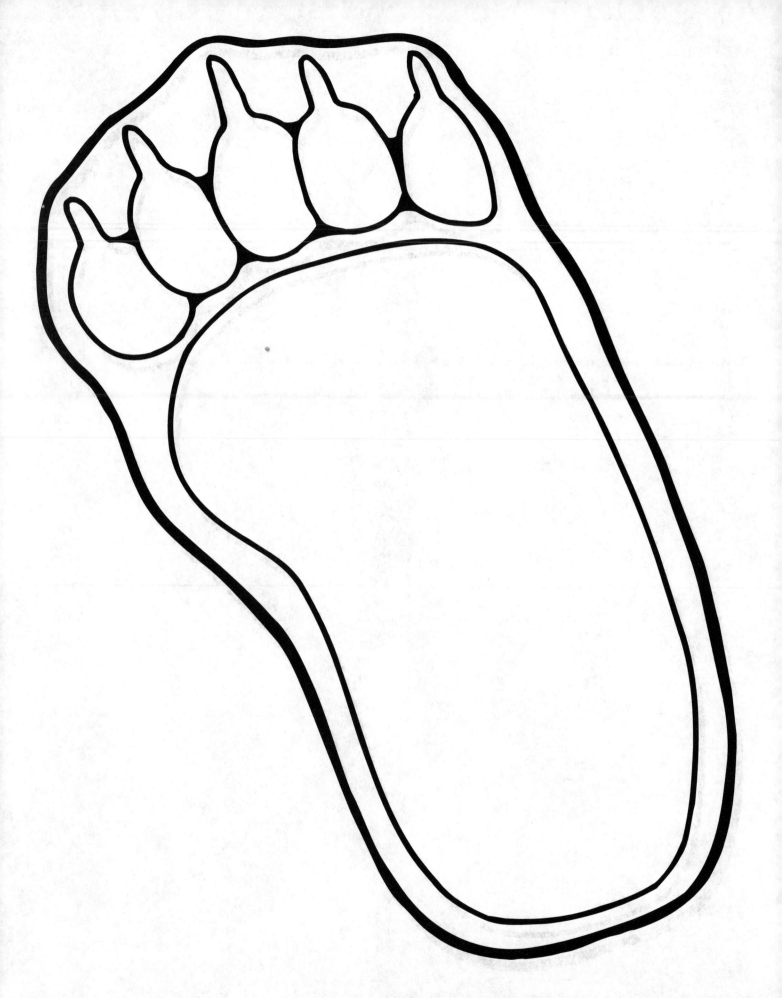

74

My most un-BEAR-able day!

Name: _____

Cut Out

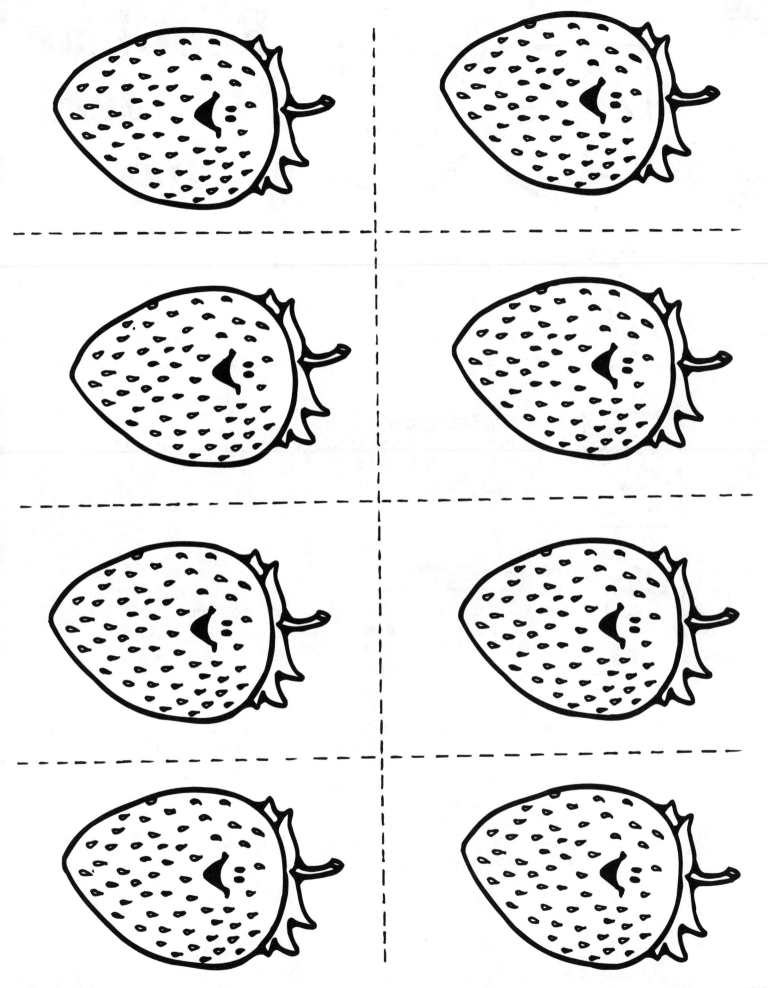

Reptilian Wonders Day

August 11

Setting the Stage

• Display toy reptiles and pictures of reptiles around related literature to gather interest in today's activities.

• Construct a semantic web with facts your students already know about reptiles and then list additional things your class wants to learn about them.

Historical Background

Today marks the birthday of Joanna Cole, a children's author who wrote *A Snake's Body*. She was born on this day in 1944.

Literary Exploration

Alligators by James Gerhold
The Boy Who Swallowed Snakes by Laurence Yep
A Child's Book of Snakes by Kathleen Daly
Crocodile and Alligator by Vincent Serventy
Crocodile Beat by Gail Jorgensen
A Gathering of Snakes by Bianca Lavies
The Girl Who Wore Snakes by Angela Johnson
The Great Snake Escape by Molly Coxe
The How and Why Wonder Book of Reptiles by Robert Mathewson
Let's Look at Reptiles by Harriet E. Huntington
Lizard in the Sun by Joanne Ryder
Lizards by James Gerhold
Lizards by Claudia Schnieper
Lizards and Other Reptiles by Edward Ricciuti
Poisonous Snakes by Seymour Simon

Literary Exploration continued

Reptiles by Beverly Armstrong
Reptiles by Lois Ballard
Reptiles by Frank Brennan
Reptiles by David Lambert
Reptiles by Jenny Markert
Reptiles by Kate Petty
Reptiles by Joy Richardson
Reptiles by Eileen Spinelli
Reptiles by Phillip Steele
Reptiles by Lynn Stone
Reptiles by John Bennett Wexo
Reptiles Do the Strangest Things by Leonora and Arthur Hornblow
Revolting Reptiles by Steve Parker
Roaring Reptiles by D. M. Souza
Ruth Heller's How to Hide a Crocodile by Ruth Heller
The Secretive Timber Rattlesnake by Bianca Lavies
Slither McCreep and His Brother, Joe by Tony Johnston
Small Green Snake by Libba Moore
Snake Hunt by Jill Kastner
Snake in, Snake Out by Linda Banchek
Snakes by James Gerhold
Snakes by Eric Grace
Snakes by Seymour Simon
Snakes and Other Reptiles by Mary Elting
Snakes and Other Reptiles by Q. L. Pearce
Snakes Are Hunters by Patricia Lauber
A Snake's Body by Joanna Cole
Take a Look at Snakes by Betsy Maestro
Turtle Day by Douglas Florian
Turtle Watch by George Ancona
What's So Funny, Ketu? by Verna Aardema
World of the Reptiles by John G. Head
The Yucky Reptile Alphabet Book by Jerry Pallotta

Language Experience

• Let students brainstorm words that rhyme with *snake*.

Reptilian Wonders

Writing Experience

• Students will enjoy writing facts they have learned about snakes, turtles crocodiles, alligators or lizards. See reproducible on page 82.

Science/Health Experience

• Today is the perfect opportunity to begin a science unit on reptiles and their habitat.

• Review safety around reptiles such as snakes.

Social Studies Experience

• Learn about where snakes live. Locate places around the country on a map such as desert areas that probably have snakes.

Music/Dramatic Experience

• Let amateur comedians perform some of the jokes from *Snakes Alive! Jokes About Snakes* written by Diane L. Burns.

• Let students perform Shel Silverstein's poem "Boa Constrictor" in *Where the Sidewalk Ends* as a choral reading.

Physical/Sensory Experience

• Have students form a line by putting their hands on the waist of the person in front of them to form a traveling "snake" around the room.

Arts/Crafts Experience

• Students can make a "moveable" snake by threading egg carton sections on a string. They can add wiggly eyes and a red construction paper forked tongue.

Extension Activities

• If you are near a zoo or museum with a reptile show, take a class field trip to see the interesting creatures up close.

• Serve miniature snakes (gummy worms) for a slithery treat.

 Reptilian Wonders

Reptilian Wonders

Reptilian Wonders

FUN FACTS ABOUT REPTILES!

Name: _____

Insectophobia Day

August 12

Setting the Stage
- Display student insect art around images of insects with the caption: "Insects Don't Bug Us!"

- Construct a semantic web with facts your students know (or want to know) about insect life.

Literary Exploration
Alpha Bugs by David Carter
Antics by Cathi Hepworth
Backyard Insects by Millicent Selsam and Ronald Goor
Benjamin's Bugs by Mary Morgan
Bugs by Mary Ann Hoberman
Bugs by Nancy Winslow Parker and Joan Richards Wright
Creepy Creatures by D. J. Arneson
Feely Bugs by David Carter
Fireflies! Story and Pictures by Julie Brinckloe
Fly Away Home by Jack Kent
The Grouchy Ladybug by Eric Carle
Hey Bug! and Other Poems About Little Things by Elizabeth Itse
How to Hide a Butterfly and Other Insects by Ruth Heller
The Hungry Caterpillar by Eric Carle
The Icky Bug Alphabet Book by Jerry Pallotta
If at First You Do Not See by Ruth Brown
Insect Metamorphosis: From Egg to Adult by Ron and Nancy Goor
Insect World by Time Life Books
Insects and Their Homes by Hidetomo Oda
Insects Are My Life by Megan McDonald
Insects Do the Strangest Things by Leonora Hornblow
Insects from Outer Space by Frank Asch

Literary Exploration continued

Ladybug by Emery Bernhard
The Ladybug and Other Insects by Pascale deBourgoing
Ladybug, Ladybug Fly Away Home by Judy Hawes
The Ladybug on the Move by Richard Fowler
Look at Insects by Roma Bishop
More Bugs in Boxes by David A. Carter
Nicholas Cricket by Joyce Maxner
Old Black Fly by Jim Aylesworth
Over the Steamy Swamp by Paul Geraghty
Two Bad Ants by Chris Van Allsburg
What About Ladybugs? by Celia Godkin
What's Inside? Insects by Dorling Kindersley
Why Mosquitoes Buzz in People's Ears by Verna Aardema

Language Experience

• How many words can your students think of that rhyme with *bug*?

Writing Experience

• Let students write about what really "bugs" them. See reproducible on page 89.

Name: _____

84

TLC10452 Copyright © Teaching & Learning Company, Carthage, IL 62321-001

Math Experience

- Have students practice sequencing numbers (by ones, twos, fives or tens) with a Counting Caterpillar. Write numbers on dry lima beans. Let students put them in sequence in the shape of a caterpillar.

- They can practice counting coins by making a Cent Centipede. Place coins in varying amounts on a table and let students count the value of the cents by forming the shape of a CENTipede.

Science/Health Experience

- Today is a perfect day to begin a science unit on insects and their habitats.

- Let cooperative groups research chosen insects and share their findings with the rest of the class.

Music/Dramatic Experience

- Have students read the traditional children's favorite, "I Know an Old Woman Who Swallowed a Fly" as a choral reading. You may prefer to read Nadine Westcott Bernard's version of *I Know an Old Woman Who Swallowed a Fly* as students chant along.

- Sing the old favorite song, "Shoo Fly, Don't Bother Me."

- Aspiring comedians might want to try a few jokes out on the class. Have them use *Going Buggy! Jokes About Insects*, written by Peter and Connie Roop.

Physical/Sensory Experience

• Take your students on an outdoor safari hunt for bugs. Make sure the bugs are put in ventilated jars with plenty of their natural habitat (leaves, sticks), then released after observation.

• Let your students get out their wiggles by creeping, flying, buzzing or fluttering like insects.

• Play the Centipede Game! Divide students into relay teams and have them line up. Each sits down behind someone wrapping their legs around that person to form a centipede's body. The team who can make it to the finish line first, still connected, wins.

• Another fun game is Caterpillar! Divide students into two equal groups. Have everyone lie facedown on the floor. The person at the head of the line rolls over the other students to the end of the line. Then the next person in line does the same thing. The game continues until everyone has had a turn.

Arts/Crafts Experience

- Let students diagram the life cycle of an insect, such as a monarch butterfly. Illustrations could include: The EGGS hatch on the milkweed plant. The CATERPILLAR eats the milkweed leaves. The caterpillar then makes a CHRYSALIS on the milkweed leaf. The chrysalis opens to reveal a beautiful orange and black monarch BUTTERFLY ready to fly.

- Provide students with craft materials and odds and ends. Challenge them to build a bug with the items, making sure to include the head, thorax and abdomen.

- A caterpillar can be made from painting egg carton sections and glueing them together. Add details such as pipe cleaner antennae and wiggly eyes.

- Ladybugs can be made by painting walnut halves with red and white acrylic paint and adding black spots.

Insectophobia
Insectophobia
Insectophobia
Insectophobia

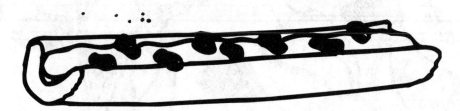

Extension Activities

- Invite an entomologist to come and talk to your students about his or her work with bugs.

- Check with nearby museums to see if they have insect display cases your students can go to see.

- Serve Grasshopper Mint Cookies or Bugs on a Log (raisins on peanut-butter covered celery).

- Let students make Edible Insects. Place raisins on a red apple half (skir side up) to make a ladybug. Use honey or peanut butter for the glue. String round cereal on thin licorice whips for a caterpillar.

Values Education Experience

- Discuss the pros and cons of using pesticides in fruit groves and vegetable gardens.

Follow-Up/Homework Idea

- Invite students to look for more insects on the way home from school.

Name: _____

International Left-Handers' Day

August 13

Setting the Stage

- Young children sometimes have a hard time distinguishing between their left and right hands. Make it easier for them by taping a paper left handprint and right handprint in the left and right corners of their desks. Place larger ones in the front of the classroom. Show your students how to form an "L" with their left hand as a reminder.

Historical Background

Years ago when children were seen to be left-handed, teachers and parents tried to make them learn to be right-handed. Today we realize either one is fine.

Literary Exploration

Jim Abbott: Left-Handed Wonder by Gregory Lee
The Left-Handed Book by Rae Lindsay
Left-Handed Kids by James T. DeKay

90

Language Experience

- Let students brainstorm a list of things that would be difficult to do with their "other" hand.

Math Experience

- Have students take a survey around the school of left-handed people. Add this information to a class bar graph.

- Let students measure to see if their left hand is the same size as their right hand (sometimes fingers are longer on one hand).

Science/Health Experience

- Study the science of the dominant hand and eye. Try some experiments with the less-dominant hand such as sharpening a pencil or opening a jar.

Social Studies Experience

- Let interested students research famous "southpaws" throughout history such as: U.S. Presidents Garfield, Truman, Ford, Bush and Clinton; leaders Napoleon and Julius Caesar; scientists Benjamin Franklin and Albert Einstein and artists Leonardo daVinci and Michelangelo.

Music/Dramatic Experience

• If you have "lefties" in your class, let them plead a case for left-hande◄ people's rights (such as: the way books are bound makes it harder fo◄ a left-hander to open them).

Physical/Sensory Experience

• Challenge students to write a handwriting assignment with the less-dominant hand.

Arts/Crafts Experience

• Let students try their "hand" at drawing or painting with their less-dominant hand.

Follow-Up/Homework Idea

• Encourage your students to take a family poll to see if everyone is the same or some have a different dominant hand.

Deep in the Rain Forest Day

August 14

Setting the Stage

• Display pictures and by-products of the rain forest around related literature to engage student's attention in the day's activities.

• Construct a semantic web with facts your students already know about the tropical rain forest. Then list additional things they would like to learn.

Historical Background

Until a couple of hundred years ago, 20% of the Earth's entire land surface was made up of rain forest. Now there is little more than 5% and more of it vanishes every day.

Literary Exploration

Feathers Like a Rainbow by Flora
The Great Kapok Tree by Lynn Cherry
Journey of the Red-Eyed Tree Frog by Martin and Tanis Jordan
Journey Through a Tropical Jungle by Adrian Forsyth
Jungles and Rainforests by Rowland Entwistle
Life in the Rainforest by Lucy Baker
Life in the Rainforest by Melvin Berger
Look inside a Rainforest by Giovanna Mantegazza
One Day in the Tropical Rainforest by Jean Craighead George
Our Endangered Planet: Tropical Rain Forests by C. Mutel
Pandas by Ruth Belov Gross
Panther Dream by Bob and Wendy Weir
Rain Forest by Helen Cowcher
The Rain Forest by Billy Goodman
Rain Forest Secrets by Arthur Dorros
Rainforest Animals by Michael Chinery
Tropical Rainforest by James D. Nations
Tropical Rainforest by Michael Bright
A Walk in the Rainforest by Kristin Pratt

Language Experience

• How many words can your students make out of the letters in *rain forest*? See reproducible on page 98.

How many new words can you make using the letters in

RAIN FOREST?

Name: _____

Writing Experience

• Borrow a CD or cassette of jungle music from the library and play it in the background as students imagine they are walking through the jungle. Ask them to write about what they see, smell and hear.

• Half of all living things on the Earth currently live in the rain forest. Most have not even been named, let alone studied. Have each student write about a new plant or animal that no one else has discovered ye Encourage them to use their imagination.

Math Experience

- Since there are so many plants and animals vanishing from our rain forests, why not pose some rain forest subtraction problems? (One day there were 7 three-toed sloths. The next day 4 were missing. How many were left? or There were 12 Proboscis Monkeys, but now there are 8. How many disappeared?)

Science/Health Experience

- Today is a great opportunity to learn about the dangerous plight of our Earth's tropical rain forests. Discuss how the elimination of trees in the rain forest creates problems for our planet. Explain that trees and plants give off oxygen which people need. They absorb carbon dioxide which people don't need. Without plants and trees, there is less oxygen and more carbon dioxide.

- Let students research products that come from the rain forests: furniture, rubber, foods and spices. Have them share their findings with the rest of the class.

- Students can research medicines that come from products in the rain forests. For example, quinine is a medicine used to treat malaria, Hodgkin's disease and Lukemia.

- Learn more about plants in the rain forest that produce rare fruit and nuts.

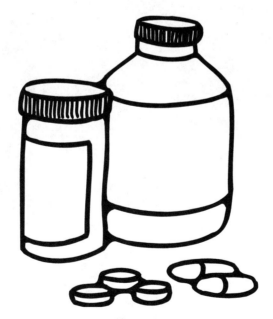

Deep
in the
Rain Forest

Deep
in the
Rain Forest

Deep
in the
Rain Forest

Social Studies Experience

• Discuss what has been happening with rain forests over the years. Explain that with deforestation we are destroying rain forests to create more space for cattle grazing, cutting down trees for additional lumber and providing space for growing population needs. Let students brain storm other ways we can deal with our needs without destroying rain forests.

Music/Dramatic Experience

• From a local library, borrow a CD or cassette of "jungle-type" music with exotic sounds.

Physical/Sensory Experience

• Play on your school "Jungle" gym today!

• Create the "feel" of the tropical rain forest by turning up the thermostat a little and running a humidifier.

Arts/Crafts Experience

• Share the art of Henri Rousseau whose exotic jungle prints are very interesting.

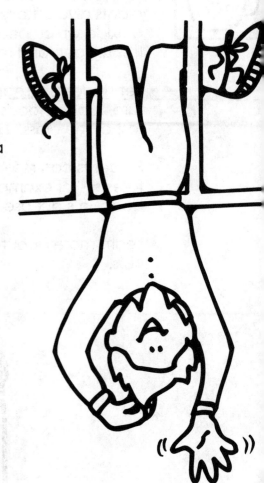

96

Extension Activities

• Create the levels of the rain forest in your classroom with a Rain Forest Mural! Students can create green crepe paper leaves for trees and plants. Label each area with basic levels: top or emergent layer, canopy, understory and forest floor. Students can draw animals, birds, insects and plants that might live in each level of the rain forest, such as: a monkey in the canopy; a jaguar and tapir in the understory and so on.

• Serve fresh tropical fruit (papaya, kiwi, mango, pineapple, coconut and banana) or nuts (such as cashews) that can be found in the rain forest.

• Serve Jungle Slush.

Jungle Slush

Mix: 2 c. pineapple juice
1 banana
1 t. coconut flavoring
ice cubes

Blend in blender until slushy.

Values Education Experience

• Review the value of taking care of our planet.

Follow-Up/Homework Idea

• Encourage students to help save trees by cutting back on paper use.

How many new words can you make using the letters in

RAIN FOREST?

Name: _____

National Relaxation Day

August 15

Setting the Stage
• Construct a semantic web with words your students think of when you say the word *relax*.

Historical Background
National Relaxation Day is not an official holiday, but August 15 is generally recognized as a day to think about and enjoy relaxation. Relaxation is a modern idea. Before the 20th century, people had to work much harder. Labor-saving devices, many of which were invited in the late 1800s and early 1900s, made it possible for people to take time to relax.

Literary Exploration
Albert the Running Bear Gets the Jitters by Barbara Isenberg
A Summer Day by Douglas Florian
Take Time to Relax by Nancy Carlson

Writing Experience

• Let students write about what they like to do to really relax when they have the time. See reproducible on page 102.

What I love to do when I can...

Name: _____

Science/Health Experience

• Talk about the need for rest and relaxation from work and stressful situations.

Social Studies Experience

• Discuss the difference between relaxation and procrastination.

Music/Dramatic Experience

• Borrow Hap Palmer's "Quiet Places" (sound recording) from a local library to play in the background while students work on their relaxing projects.

Physical/Sensory Experience
- Play Hurry. Make sure students notice the difference between playing the game and the few moments of relaxation afterward. Talk about the differences.

How to Play
Divide the class into two teams and designate which half of the playing field or gym area they stay in. Provide a dividing line between them (even if it's just a rope). Give each team five or six balls. At a signal, each team hurries to get the balls away from their side by throwing them to the opposite side. When the ending whistle is blown, the balls are counted and the side with the fewest, wins.

- Teach students basic relaxation techniques such as deep breathing, counting slowly or peaceful images and thoughts.

Arts/Crafts Experience
- Let students paint quietly while listening to relaxing music.

Follow-Up/Homework Idea
- Tell your students that their homework assignment is to go home and take it easy!

What I love to do when I can...

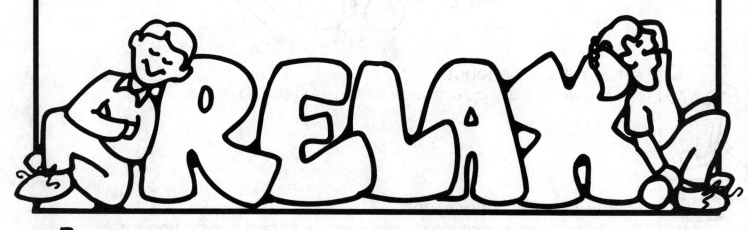

Name: _____

Teddy Bear Picnic Day

August 16

Setting the Stage

- Display student work around a picture of a teddy bear with the caption: "BEAR-Y Good Work!" or book jacket covers with the caption: "Reading Makes Life BEARable!"

- Begin a campaign for reading with a B.E.A.R. (Be Excited About Reading) kickoff! Encourage students to "paws" each day to read at home, asking parents to initial a calendar to show their reading. Calendar and sticker patterns on pages 107-108.

- Invite each student to bring a teddy bear or favorite stuffed animal to school today.

- Display plenty of toy, stuffed teddy bears around related literature to get students excited about the day.

- Hand out bear-shaped treats, gummy bears or Teddy Grahams™, at various times throughout the day.

Literary Exploration

Bear by Himself by Geoffrey Hayes
Bear Party by William duBois
Bear's Bargain by Frank Asch
Bear's Shadow by Frank Asch
Corduroy by Don Freeman
Day Care Teddy Bear by True Kelley
Edward Loses His Teddy Bear by Michaela Morgan
The First Teddy Bear by Helen Kay
Floppy Teddy Bear by Patricia Lillie
Good as New by Barbara Douglass
Ira Sleeps Over by Bernard Waber
Jesse Bear, What Will You Wear? by Nancy White Carlstrom
Little Bear (Series) by Else Homelund Minarik
A Little Book of Teddy Bear Tales by Juliette Clark
Marcus & Lionel by Ronne P. Randall
My Teddy Bear by Chiyoko Nakantani
Old Bear by Jane Hissey
One Little Teddy Bear by Mark Burgess
Paddington by Michael Bond
Sam's Teddy Bear by Barbro Lindgren
Teddy by Enid Romanek
The Teddy Bear Book by Jean Marzollo
Teddy Bear Cures a Cold by Susanna Gretz
Teddy Bear, Teddy Bear by Marc Brown
Teddy Bear's Picnic by Jimmy Kennedy
Teddy Bears 1 to 10 by Susanna Gretz
Teddy Bear, Teddy Bear by Michael Hague
The Teddy Bear Who Couldn't Do Anything by Dina Anastasio
What a Teddy Bear Needs by Marilyn Kaye
Winnie the Pooh by A.A. Milne

104

Language Experience

• How many words can your students come up with that rhyme with *bear*?

Writing Experience

• Read aloud the book, *What a Teddy Bear Needs* by Marilyn Kaye. Have students be Teddy Bear Experts and write about how to care for a teddy bear.

Music/Dramatic Experience

• Younger students can pretend they are cuddly teddy bears. Let them make headbands from brown construction paper. They could even act out the story of "Goldilocks and the Three Bears." See patterns on page 109.

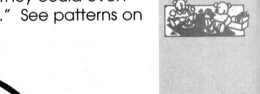

Teddy Bear Picnic

• Let interested students perform comedy stand-up routines using jokes from *Grin and Bear It: Jokes About Teddy Bears* written by Sharon Friedman.

• Check out a sound recording of "The Teddy Bear's Picnic" by Gary Rosen or "Rock 'n' Roll Teddy Bear" by Rosenshontz from a local library for students to listen to.

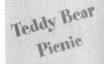

Physical/Sensory Experience

• Let students play Teddy, Teddy, Bear a variation of Duck, Duck, Goose. They chase "it" when they are tapped with the word *bear*.

• Students will enjoy playing Hot Potato in a new way as they sit in a circle passing around a teddy bear. When the music stops, whoever is holding the bear is out. Eventually only one person will be left.

Arts/Crafts Experience

• Have students make teddy bears from brown construction paper, adding button eyes, a red pom-pom nose and yarn mouth. They can be stuffed with crumpled paper for a three-dimensional effect.

Extension Activities

• Host a Teddy Bear Picnic! Invite everyone to bring a teddy bear or stuffed animal to school. Set the teddy bears around a picnic area at a local park, the playground or your classroom. Have contests with the bears (biggest, smallest, best-dressed, most loved or worn, newest). Present award ribbons. Serve Teddy Grahams™ and "beary" juice (berry juice). Read aloud the story *The Teddy Bear's Picnic* by Jimmy Kennedy. See award patterns on page 110.

• Make a Teddy Bear cake. Bake a round cake and ice it with chocolate frosting. Add ears of chocolate marshmallow cookies or cupcakes. Eyes can be made with vanilla wafers or chocolate cookie centers surrounded by white icing. The bear's snout is made from a big chocolate muffin. Details inside the ears and on the snout can be added by piping thin lines of chocolate frosting or using thin licorice. Add another round cake for the teddy bear body with cookie buttons down the front and ladyfinger cookies for arms and legs. Your students will love it!

Follow-Up/Homework Idea

• Remind students to take their teddy bears home and take good care of them!

Be Excited About Reading

Month:

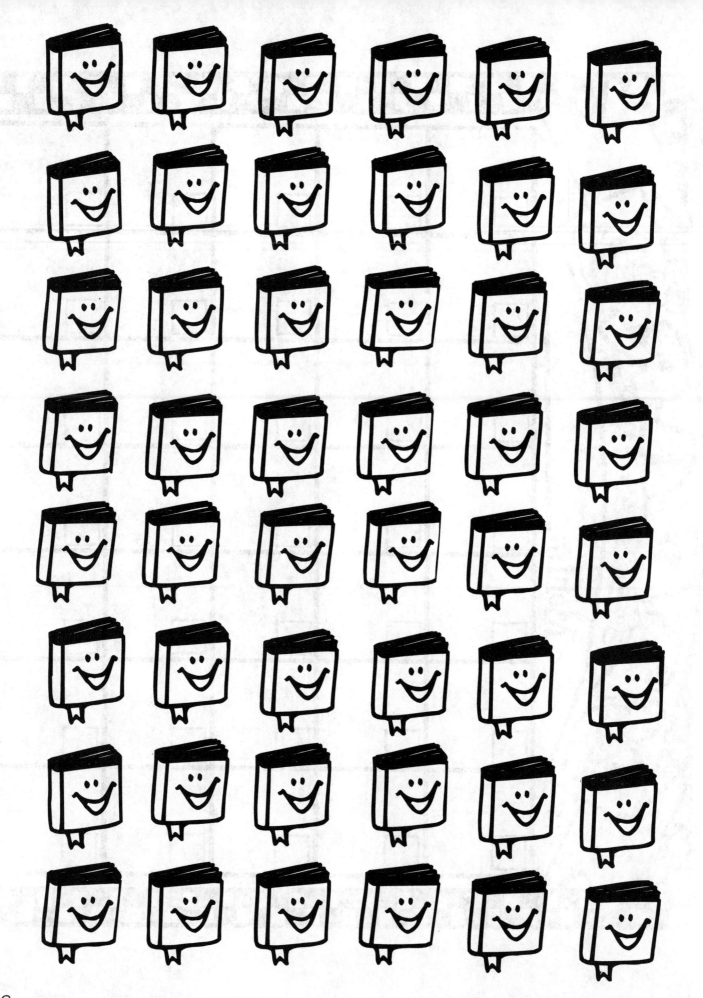

108

B

Glue to A.

Glue to B.

A

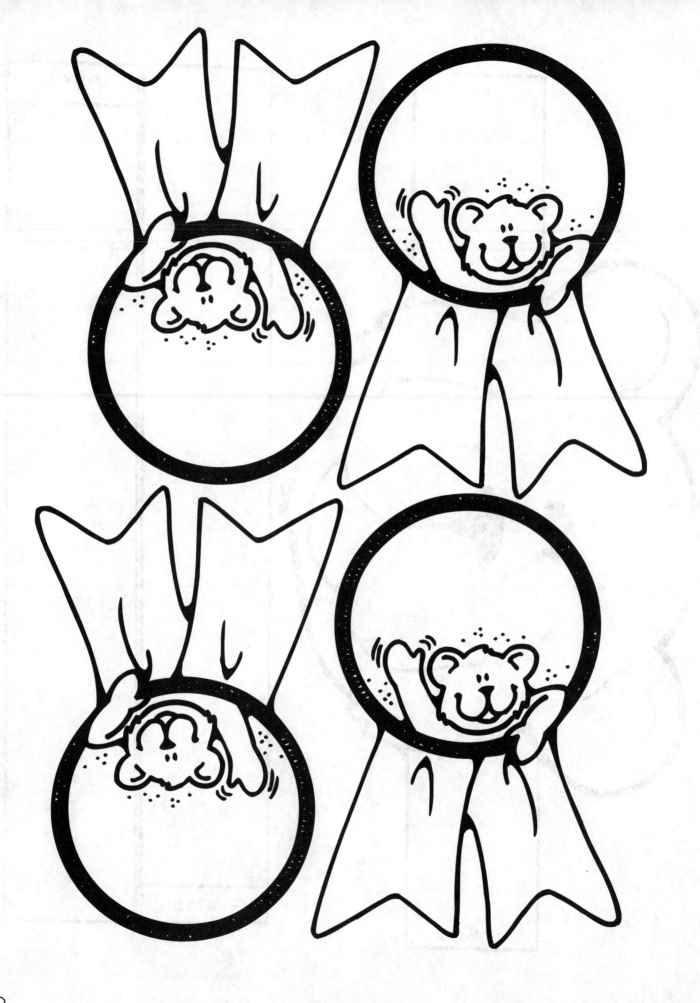

Turtle Toodleoo Day

August 17

Setting the Stage

- Set up pictures of turtles (as well as toy turtles) around related literature to add interest about today's emphasis.

- Construct a semantic web with facts your students already know (or would like to know) about turtles and tortoises.

Literary Exploration

Esio Trot by Roald Dahl
The Foolish Tortoise and the Greedy Python by Richard Buckley
Franklin Is Bossy (series) by Paulette Bourgeois
A Home for Little Turtle by Ariane Chottin
I Can't Get My Turtle to Move by Elizabeth Lee O'Donnell
M.C. Turtle and the Hip Hop Hare by David Vozar
In the Middle of the Puddle by Mike Thaler
The Moonrat and the White Turtle by Helen Ward
Old Turtle by Douglas Wood
Rosebud by Ed Emberley
The Smallest Turtle by Lynley Dodd
And Still the Turtle Watched by Sheila MacGill
Theodore Turtle by Ellen MacGregor
Three Tales of Turtle by Ruth Tooze
Timothy Turtle by Alice Davis
Timothy Turtle by Al Graham
Tiny Timothy Turtle by Anna Leditschke
Tortoise and the Hare by Janet Stevens
Turtle and the Dove by Don Freeman
The Turtle and the Moon by Charles Turner
Turtle and Tortoise by Vincent Serventy
The Turtle Book by Mel Crawford
Turtle Day by Douglas Florian
Turtle Tale by Frank Asch
Turtle Time by Sandol Stoddard
Turtles and Tortoises by James Gerholdt
What Is a Turtle? by Gene Darby
Yertle the Turtle and Other Stories by Dr. Suess

Science/Health Experience

• Study turtles and tortoises and their habitats.

Social Studies Experience

• Learn about the history of turtles. Your students may not be aware tha turtles have been around since the dinosaurs.

• Locate the Galapagos Islands off the coast of Ecuador, and talk abou the Galapagos tortoises that live there.

Music/Dramatic Experience

• Let any interested students "come out of their shell" and act out the fable of "The Tortoise and the Hare."

Physical/Sensory Experience

• Check with a local pet shop to see if your class can borrow a couple o turtles for a good cause today. Divide the class into teams (according to how many turtles you have) and have a turtle race. Invite students to coach and cheer their team turtle over the finish line.

Arts/Crafts Experience

- Create homemade turtles! Have students paint paper plates and add legs, a head and a tail. See patterns for legs, head and tail on page 114.

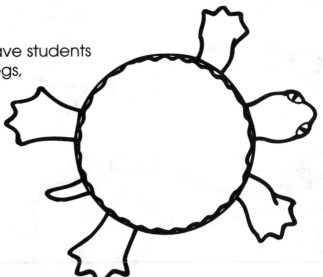

Extension Activities

- If you know someone who has a turtle, invite the person to bring it to your class and talk about how to care for a it.

- If you are near a pet show that includes turtles, take your class to it for a field trip.

- Try making chocolate turtles!

Chocolate Turtles

Melt: 1/2 cup margarine, 2 squares unsweetened chocolate. Set aside.

Add in: 2 beaten eggs, 3/4 cup sugar. Combine all ingredients.

Fold in: 1 cup flour, 1 teaspoon vanilla.

Drop by teaspoonful onto a hot waffle maker.

Follow-Up/Homework Idea

- Encourage students not to be slow as turtles, but quickly get home after school.

113

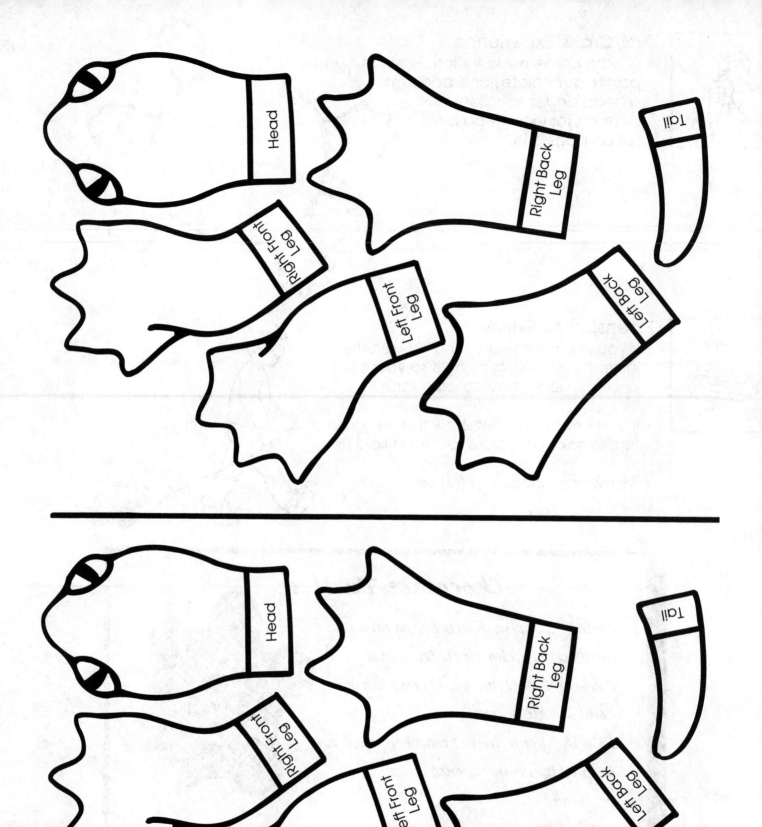

Head

Right Back
Leg

Tail

Right Front
Leg

Left Front
Leg

Left Back
Leg

Head

Right Back
Leg

Tail

Right Front
Leg

Left Front
Leg

Left Back
Leg

114

Camping Day

August 18

Setting the Stage

- Make an authentic-looking campfire by placing a searchlight bulb (lantern) under yellow and red transparent cellophane (gels). Add thin sticks vertically around the center and wood logs around those (horizontally). Add a ring of large, smooth rocks around the logs. This will give your classroom a "campy" atmosphere. Display literature about camping all around the campfire. Student desks can be arranged in a circle around the campfire.

- Set a tent up in one corner of your classroom. Let students earn the right to go inside and read camp-related literature with a flashlight. A display of a backpack, sleeping bag, outdoor canteen and cooking supplies will complete the scene.

Setting the Stage continued

- Display student work around a picture of a campfire with the caption: "How Does Our Work Stack Up?"

- Display authentic-looking animal tracks such as coyote or bear or a tro marked with sticks and arrows leading to your classroom. Put a sign made of craft sticks on the door: "CAMP HIA-_____ (fill in teacher's name).

- Wear khakis and hiking boots, visor or baseball cap and a whistle around your neck to greet your "campers." Assign a student to gathe everyone for roll call to begin your day at "camp"!

- Construct a semantic web with facts your students know (or want to know) about camping.

Historical Background

On this day in 1873, some hikers and climbers are credited with being the first ever to reach the top of Mount Whitney, the highest peak in the U.S.

Literary Exploration

Amelia Bedelia Goes Camping by Peggy Parish
Arnie Goes to Camp by Nancy Carlson
Arthur Goes to Camp by Marc Brown
Arthur's Campout by Lillian Hoban
Bailey Goes to Camp by Kevin Henkes
The Berenstain Bears Go to Camp by Stan Berenstain
Camp Big Paw by Doug Cushman
Camp Keewee's Secret Weapon by Janet Schulmap
Camp Rotten Time by Mike Thaler
Camping by Keith Pigdon
Curious George Goes Camping by Margret Rey
Did You Hear Something? Slightly Spooky Campfire Stories by Michael
   Teitelbaum
Dinosaurs Beware! A Safety Guide to Camping by Marc Brown
Do Not Disturb by Nancy Tafuri
Escape from Camp Wannabarf by Peter Hannan
First Book of Camp by Edward Janes
Garfield Goes Camping by Jim Davis
Huff and Puff Go to Camp by Jean Warren
I Don't Want to Go to Camp by Eve Bunting
Just Camping Out by Mercer Mayer
Just Me and My Dad by Mercer Mayer
Little Critter and Scout Camp by Mercer Mayer
My Mom Made Me Go to Camp by Judy Delton
On Our Vacation by Anne Rockwell
Petey Moroni's Camp Runamok Diary by Pat Cummings
Pig Pig Goes to Camp by David McPhail
Pinky and Rex Go to Camp by James Howe
Ronald Morgan Goes to Camp by Patricia Reilly Giff
Webster and Arnold Go Camping by P.K. Roche
When I Go Camping with Grandma by Marion Bauer

Language Experience

• Let students brainstorm words that rhyme with *camp*.

Writing Experience

• Let students write postcards "home" telling about imaginary camp experiences. See postcard patterns on page 121.

• Tell students they can only take five things with them in their backpacks to camp. What five things will they take and why?

Science/Health Experience

• Review safety precautions when camping. Share from Marc Brown's *Dinosaurs Beware! A Safety Guide to Camping*.

• Study basic survival skills. If possible, share a camping survival kit with items such as first aid equipment, fishing line, iodine tablets, whistle, energy bar, waterproof matches and compass. Discuss what these items are used for.

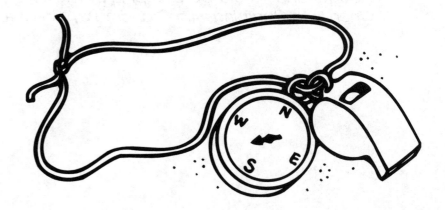

• Review campsite care and reinforce the need to care for our Earth's resources and preserve its natural beauty. Encourage students not to litter but pick up the litter they find, not to use soaps and detergents near streams or lakes, keep on assigned camping trails and leave a clean area when finished.

Social Studies Experience
- Locate on a map famous campsites, such as Yosemite and Yellowstone, and national parks around the country.

Music/Dramatic Experience
- Borrow sound recordings from *Camp Songs with 6 to 11 Year Olds* by Pete Seeger or *Songs of Camp* by Ed Badeaux from a local library to play for your students.

- Check out camp songs from Nicki Weiss' songbook *If You're Happy and You Know It*. Sing the songs around your mock campfire. If possible, have an adult accompany you on a guitar.

Physical/Sensory Experience
- Invite a local Boy Scout leader or teen Scout to teach your students some basic knot tying, such as those used to secure tents or hitch a line to a post.

- Students will enjoy an old-fashioned game of Tug-of-War.

- Camp wouldn't be camp without exercises! Lead students in jumping jacks, pushups and other muscle-stretching activities.

Arts/Crafts Experience
- Involve students in camp crafts such as metal crafts, woodworking, needlecrafts, leatherworks, nature collages or paintings inspired by the great outdoors!

Extension Activities
- Why not have simulated camp experiences? A *Boy Scout Handbook* can give you a lot of ideas. Try a morning cookout, camp crafts, scavenger hunt, putting on skits and singing or telling scary stories while making s'mores.

Extension Activities continued

S'Mores

Place a chocolate bar square on a graham cracker half. Lay a large marshmallow on top of the chocolate bar. Melt these in a toaster oven until chocolate and marshmallow start to melt into each other. Remove from the toaster oven and place the other half of the graham cracker on top. Then enjoy!

• What do you serve hungry campers? Why Pigs in a Sleeping Bag of course, hot dogs wrapped in a bedroll of refrigerated biscuit.

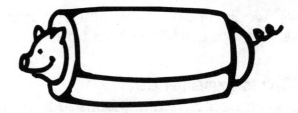

• Serve trail mix (peanuts, raisins, seeds, m & ms®, dried fruit and pretzels) or S'Mores™ cereal for a fun snack!

Values Education Experience

• Discuss the value of understanding basic skills when we are out of our natural element.

Follow-Up/Homework Idea

• Encourage students to plan a family campout with their families, even it's in their own backyard.

Desert Day

August 19

Setting the Stage

• Display student work samples with a picture of a coyote and a desert background. Add the caption: "We're Off to a HOWLING Good Start!

Historical Background

Today marks the birthday of Vicki Cobb, author of *This Place Is Dry: Arizona's Sonoran Desert*, born on this day in 1938.

Literary Exploration

Alejandro's Gift by Richard Albert
All About the Desert by Sam Epstein
Animals of the Desert by John Cloudsley-Thompson
Bluejay in the Desert by Marlene Shigekawa
Coyote Dreams by Susan Nunes
Dance in the Desert by Madeleine L'Engle
The Desert Alphabet Book by Jerry Pallotta
Desert Animals by Michael Chinery
Desert Animals by Luise Woelflein
*Desert Giant: The World of the Saguaro
   Cactus* by Barbara Bash
The Desert Is Theirs by Byrd Baylor
Desert Life by Ruth Kirk
Desert Life by Barbara Taylor
Desert People by Ann Nolan Clark
Desert Voices by Byrd Baylor
Desert: The Living World by Clive Catchpole
Deserts by Martin Bramwell
Deserts by Seymour Simon
Discover My World: Desert by Ron Hirschi
Here Is the Southwestern Desert by
   Madeleine Dunphy
The Hidden Life of the Desert by Thomas
   Wiewandt

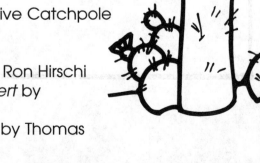

122

Literary Exploration continued

In the Desert by Gail Stewart
Life in the Deserts by Lucy Baker
Listen to the Desert by Pat Mora
Living in the Desert by John Cloudsley-Thompson
A Night and Day in the Desert by Jennifer Owings Dewey
One Night: A Story from the Desert by Cristina Kessler
One Small Square: Cactus Desert by Donald M. Silver
Survival! In the Desert by Susan Landsman
This Place Is Dry: Arizona's Sonoran Desert by Vicki Cobb
What Is a Desert? by Chris Arvetis
Wonders of the Desert World by Judith Rinard

Language Experience

• Review the use of a pronunciation guide and key when deciding the confusing context of a word. For example, depending on the way a word like *desert* is pronounced, it can be read as a noun (a place) or a verb (to abandon).

Writing Experience

• Let students imagine they are alone in a desert without any water. Ask them to write their thoughts. See reproducible on page 126.

If I were all alone in the desert with no water, I would....

Name: _____

Science/Health Experience

• Study the desert as a habitat and the plants and animals that flourish there. Visit the livingdesert.org web site for educational information and photos.

Social Studies Experience

• Locate on a world map some major deserts, such as the Gobi, Sahara, Arabian, North American and Australian Deserts.

Music/Dramatic Experience

• Enlist a several students to participate in a humorous skit. Have them drag themselves across the floor begging for water. Eventually, when they reach the other side of the room, they look excited at finding water. They quickly stand, pull out imaginary combs from their pockets, dip them in the water and start slicking back their hair. Students love it!

124

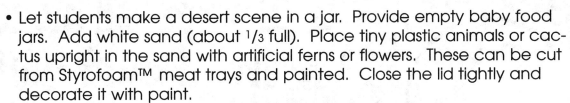

Arts/Crafts Experience

- As a class, study the desert paintings of Georgia O'Keeffe.

- Let students make a desert scene in a jar. Provide empty baby food jars. Add white sand (about ⅓ full). Place tiny plastic animals or cactus upright in the sand with artificial ferns or flowers. These can be cut from Styrofoam™ meat trays and painted. Close the lid tightly and decorate it with paint.

- Students can create their own desert pictures. Have them paint a watercolor sunset with warm colors. Let it dry. Then have them cut a cactus shape from black construction paper and glue it on the watercolor painting. The result will be a desert sunset scene!

Extension Activities

- Invite someone who has lived in a desert to visit your class and share what life-style changes need to be made to adapt to the hot, dry climate.

Follow-Up/Homework Idea

- Encourage students to be sure and drink their daily requirement of six to eight glasses of water.

If I were all alone in the desert with no water, I would.....

Name: _____

Sunflower Sensations Day

August 20

Setting the Stage

• Display pictures of sunflowers around related literature to foster excitement in the day's activities.

• Leave a trail of sunflower seeds leading into your classroom.

• Create an ongoing display of a tall sunflower and a measuring stick or two. Caption this area: "We're Growing Like Weeds . . . or Sunflowers!" Let students measure each other and record their names and heights several times throughout the year to check on their growth.

• Construct a semantic web with facts your students already know (or would like to know) about sunflowers.

Historical Background

A protective Plant Quarantine Act was issued on this day in 1912. This was to restrict plants from coming into the United States from other countries. Luckily, the beautiful sunflower plant was already here!

Literary Exploration

Backyard Sunflower by Elizabeth King
The Big Seed by Ellen Howard
Camille and the Sunflowers by Laurence Anholt
Peat Moss & Ivy's Backyard Adventure by Michael Berenstain
Sunflower by Miela Ford
The Sunflower by Miles MacGregor
Sunflower House by Eve Bunting
Sunflower! by Martha McKeen Welch
A Sunflower as Big as the Sun by Shan Ellentuck
And a Sunflower Grew by Aileen Fisher
Sunflower: My Backyard Giant by Mary Sawicki
Sunflowers by Cynthia Overbeck
Sunflowers by Kathleen Pohl
Wild, Wild Sunflower Child Anna by Nancy
   White Carlstrom

Language Experience

• *Sunflower* is a compound word. Review others.

Writing Experience

• Throw a couple of seeds out the window as Jack did in "Jack in the Beanstalk." Let students write an adventure story about the result of those seeds taking root outside your window. See reproducible on page 131.

What happened to those **SEEDS?**

Name:

Math Experience

• Let students use sunflower seeds as math manipulatives to practice counting, adding and subtracting skills.

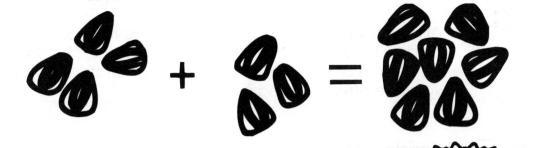

Science/Health Experience

• Do your students know that most sunflowers grow to be from two to ten feet in height? Try sprouting some sunflower seeds right in your own classroom.

Social Studies Experience

• Study the history of sunflowers in this country. Native Americans used to grow sunflower plants for food and oil. Sunflowers are not only pretty to look at but they are useful, too!

Music/Dramatic Experience

• Create a sunflower seed path (like the Yellow Brick Road) in your classroom. Students can follow the path and sing, "Follow the Sunflower Seeds!"

Arts/Crafts Experience

• Let students create a tall sunflower with a green construction paper stem and gold crepe paper petals on a paper plate face featuring sunflower seeds for the mouth, nose and eyes.

• Although Vincent Van Gogh never achieved notoriety or wealth from his art while he was alive, one of his paintings, "Sunflowers," was sold f 39.9 million dollars in 1987. Discuss other artists whose work has becom valuable after their deaths.

Extension Activities

• Serve sunflower seeds for a yummy snack!

• Let students make an Edible Sunflower by spreading cream cheese or top of a muffin. Fan out candy corn "petals" around the edges. The can also spread peanut butter on a rice cake and add sunflower seeds to the top.

Follow-Up/Homework Idea

• Challenge students to learn about other flowers and their qualities. Some flowers are edible, some are used in medicine, other are poisonous—create a bulletin board display of "Flower Facts."

What happened to those SEEDS?

Name: _____

Hawaii Statehood Day

August 21

Setting the Stage

- Encourage students to dress "Island-style" today in colorful, casual, loose-fitting clothing representative of the Hawaiian culture. Wear colorful clothes such as a muu muu and a lei around your neck. If possible, greet each student with an "Aloha" and put a lei around each one's neck. This is a Hawaiin expression of friendship and love.

- Play Hawaiian music softly in the background.

Historical Background

Hawaii was proclaimed the 50th state in the Union on this day in 1959. Statehood bill passed congress in March 1959 and signed by Ike. June 27, 1959, Hawaii voted 17 to 1 to join the Union.

Arts/Crafts Experience

- Try making grass skirts. Students staple long green palm tree leaves or paper leaf shapes to a band fitted to the waist.

- Hawaiian leis can be made with tissue or construction paper flowers strung on yarn. Add drinking straw pieces between the flowers. See flower patterns on page 136.

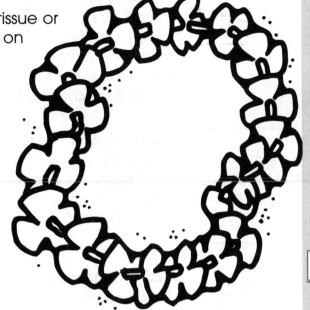

- Let students make a salt-dough relief model of the islands of Hawaii.

- Use pattern on page 135 to create a chain of Hawaiian dancers.

Extension Activities

- Invite people who have visited Hawaii to come to your class to share interesting things about it and bring items representative of this island state.

- Host a Hawaiian luau. Hawaiians typically sit on the floor with food on large green leaves for a tablecloth. Invite Polynesian dancers to your luau or play Hawaiian music and serve pineapple (Hawaii's chief product), bananas, papayas and coconut for tropical treats. Top it off with chocolate-covered macadamia nuts and Polynesian punch (add coconut flavoring to punch). Put a palm tree or little umbrella (found in novelty stores) in the punch to make it more festive.

Literary Exploration

A Is for Aloha by Stephanie Feeney
A Child's History of Hawaii by Edward J. McGrath Jr.
Hawaii by Allan Carpenter
Hawaii by Dennis B. Fradin
Hawaii by Joyce Johnston
Hawaii by William Russell
Hawaii by Kathleen Thompson
Hawaii Is a Rainbow by Stephanie Feeney

Social Studies Experience

- Study the land of Hawaii, its people and culture. Locate it on a map and point out the areas where there are volcanoes. The largest volcano in the world (two miles wide) is on the island of Maui. It has been silent so far.

Music/Dramatic Experience

- Borrow a sound recording of "Hawaii" by Harry Kalapana from a local library. Play the Hawaiian sounds and music to set the mood in your classroom.

Physical/Sensory Experience

- Invite someone who knows how to hula dance to visit your class and teach students some basic hula moves.

Values Education Experience

- Your students may not realize that only about 1% of the population of Hawaii is pure Hawaiian. Hawaii is as diverse in its population as it is beautiful. Discuss the value of diversity and the beauty in variety.

Follow-Up/Homework Idea

- Encourage students to teach the hula to their families!

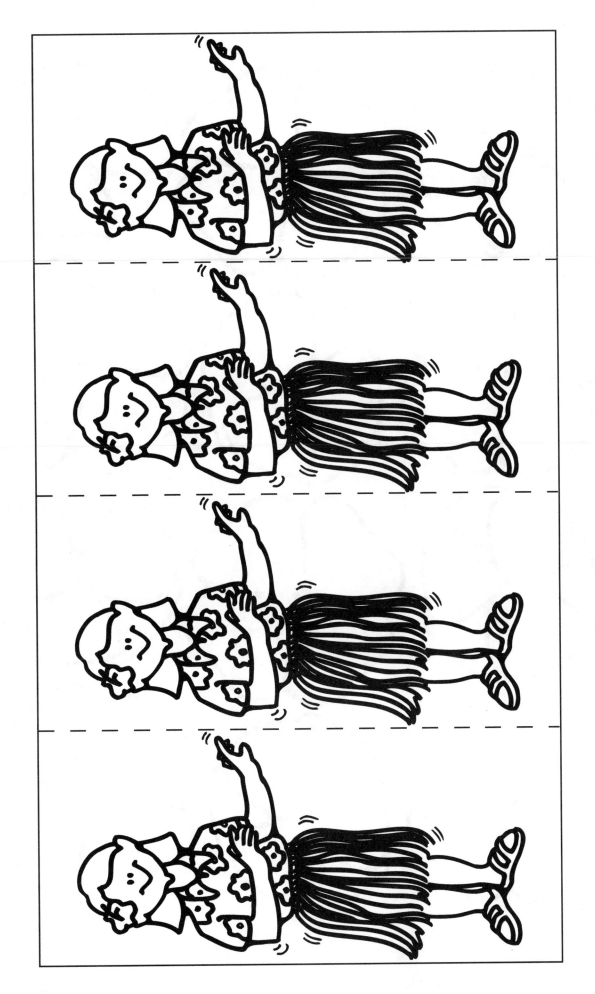

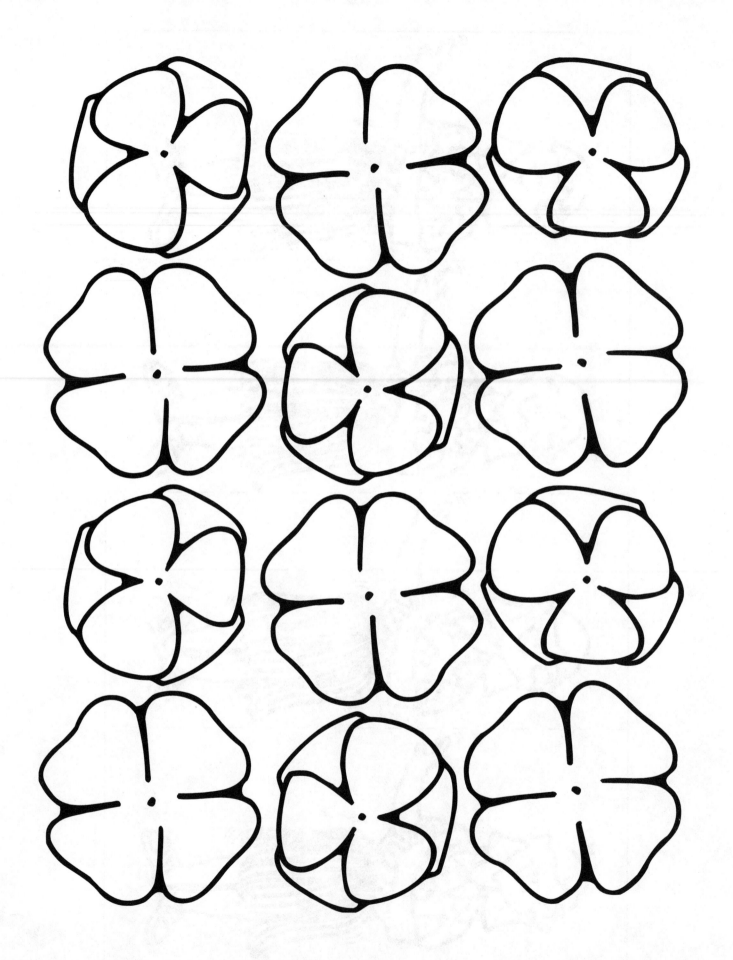

136

Career Day

August 22

Setting the Stage

- Display pictures of community workers around related literature.

- Construct a semantic web with words your students think of when you say, *career*.

Literary Exploration

Butcher, Baker, Cabinetmaker: Photographs of Women at Work by Wendy Saul

Daddies, What They Do All Day by Helen Puner

Dear Garbage Man by Gene Zion

I Want to Be a Baker by Carla Green

I Want to Be a Librarian by Donna Baker

I Want to Be a Police Officer by Donna Baker

I Want to Be . . . series, published by Children's Press

Jobs by Ross Petras

Our Friendly Helpers by Jane Hefflefinger

Postmen by Evelyn Hastings

A Story About Why People Do Different Kinds of Work by Marie Winn

The True Book of Policeman and Fireman by Irene Miner

What Is a Community? by Caroline Arnold

When I Grow Up by Anne Rockwell

Who Keeps Us Healthy? by Caroline Arnold

Who Keeps Us Safe? by Caroline Arnold

Language Experience

• Let students brainstorm kinds of community workers, then alphabetize the job titles.

Career

Writing Experience

• Give students an opportunity to reflect on what careers they have an interest in pursuing when they grow up. Have them write about their future jobs. See reproducible on page 142.

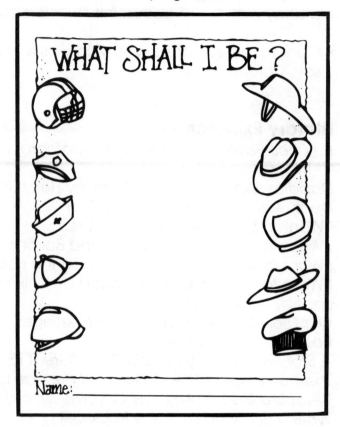

WHAT SHALL I BE?

Name: _____

• Let students write dialogue or comments that a particular community worker might say "on the job." Example: doctor—"Where does it hurt?" "Please open your mouth and say, Ah."

Career

Math Experience

• Let students take a poll around the school to find out what other students want to be when they grow up. This information can be made into a bar graph.

Career

Science/Health Experience

• Explore career possibilities in the science and health fields.

Social Studies Experience

• Today is a great opportunity to discuss various career choices and options students have in the future.

Music/Dramatic Experience

• Explore career choices in entertainment.

• Let students interview school workers asking what they do and how they feel about their work.

• Let students dress up and role-play various career options.

Physical/Sensory Experience

• Explore careers in sports and labor fields.

• Play a pantomiming game of Career Charades!

Arts/Crafts Experience

- Let students illustrate their choice of career (See reproducible on page 143.). Then let them fold their picture into thirds (horizontally) and cut on the folds. They can add their pictures to three designated piles (heads, torsos, legs and feet). Students can have fun trying to match up silly and realistic-looking career workers.

- If you have access to pictures of your students (perhaps leftover from picture day), let students cut a hole in a piece of art paper to frame the picture of their face (peeping through from behind). Then students can draw a picture of a career possibility and write the reasons for the interest in this career choice.

Extension Activities
• Host a Career Day Open House! Invite parents to come talk about their careers. Invite local community workers to come and share their expertise and work experience with your class.

Values Education Experience
• Discuss the value in having different interests and talents.

Follow-Up/Homework Idea
• Encourage students to talk to their parents about their life's work and why they do what they do.

WHAT SHALL I BE ?

Name: _____

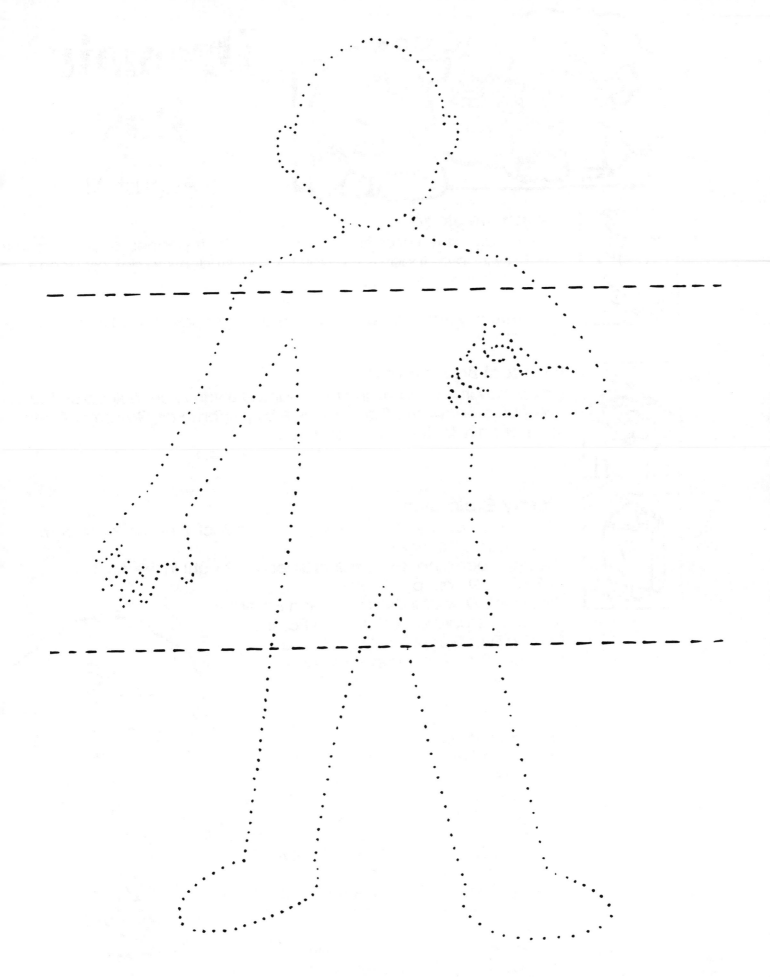

Dreamin' Day

August 23

Setting the Stage

• Encourage daydreaming today! Let students ponder, reflect and stare out a window. Today is the day for your students to get lost (then found) in their imagination!

• Construct a semantic web with words your students think of when you say the word *dreams*.

Historical Background

On this day in 1977, a young man named Bryan Allen took off on the first ever human-powered flight. He flew by pedaling his *Gossamer Condor* for about a mile. The power of dreams!

Literary Exploration

"Dreams" poem by Langston Hughes from Jack Prelutsky's *Random House Book of Poetry*
"Frozen Dream" poem from Shel Silverstein's *Light In the Attic*
Aekyung's Dream by Min Paek
Benjamin's Dreadful Dream by Alan Baker
Bridge to Terabithia by Katherine Paterson
Did You Ever Dream? by Doris Herold Lund
Dreamcatcher by Audrey Osofsky
The Dream Child by David McPhail
Dreaming by Bobette McCarthy
Dreams by Ezra Jack Keats
Dreams by Peter Spier
The Dream Tree by Stephen Cosgrove
Just a Dream by Chris Van Allsburg
The Little Engine That Could by Watty Piper
Lottie's Dream by Bonnie Pryor
The Man Who Had No Dream by Adelaide Holl
Rainy Day Dreams by Michael Chesworth
A River Dream by Allen Say
Sweet Dreams for Sally by Amelia Hubert
The Secret Garden by Frances Hodgson Burnett
The Sweetest Fig by Chris Van Allsburg
Wolf Who Had a Wonderful Dream by Anne Rockwell

Language Experience

• Let students brainstorm what people wonder about (why fire is red or when cures for so many diseases will be discovered, and so on).

Writing Experience

• Do your students dream of their futures and the futures of others? Do they wonder about the future of our planet? Let them write what they wonder. Seal the paper in an envelope, take it home and put it away to read at a later time. See reproducible on page 147.

• Have students write about one of these story starters:

The best thing that could possibly happen to me is . . .
My favorite thing to daydream about is . . .
I really wish I could . . .
If I could do anything I wanted to, I would . . .

Social Studies Experience

• If you have access to a Native American "dream-catcher," show it to your students. Explain its origin and what significance it plays in the lives of some people.

Values Education Experience

• Discuss the value and power of the imagination in creating and achieving our dreams.

Follow-Up/Homework Idea

• Encourage students to take home the papers they wrote, put them in sealed envelopes and have their parents save them for a later date. Challenge students to try to make their dreams come true!

Date: _____ Name: _____

I wonder.......

Magnificent Manners Day

August 24

Setting the Stage
• Construct a semantic web with the things your students think of when you say the word *manners*.

Historical Background
This is a perfect time to review courtesy and manners with your students.

Literary Exploration
After You by Janet Riehecky
Alligators Are Awful by David M. McPhail
Be Kind to Your Guest by Joy Berry
Do I Have to Say Hello? by Delia Ephron
Excuse Me by Janet Riehecky
I Can Read About Good Manners by Erica Frost
I'm Sorry by Janet Riehecky
Let's Talk About Being Rude by Joy Wilt Berry
Manners by Aliki
Manners by Shelly Nielsen
Manners Matter by Norah Smaridge
May I? by Janet Riehecky
Mind Your Manners! by Peggy Parish
Monster Manners by Joanna Cole
Muppet Manners by Pat Relf
Pass the Peas Please by Anastasia
Perfect Percy by Bonnie Pryor
Perfect Pigs: An Introduction to Manners by Marc Brown
Please by Janet Riehecky
Please and Thank You Book by Richard Scarry
Stand Up, Shake Hand, Say "How Do You Do?" by Marjabelle Stewart
Thank You by Janet Riehecky
The Thingamajig Book of Manners by Irene Keller
What Do You Say, Dear? by Sesyle Joslin
Woody, Be Good: A First Book of Manners by Margo Lundell

148

Language Experience

• Encourage your students to use polite vocabulary. Discuss what the words mean. Don't assume that all students have been taught polite words or the reason for them.

Writing Experience

• Have students write about why it is important to treat others with courtesy and respect. See reproducible on page 151.

Social Studies Experience

• Today is a perfect day to begin a unit on manners!

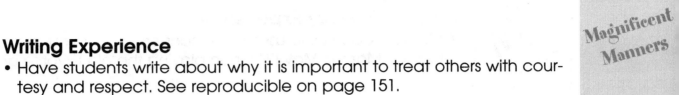

Music/Dramatic Experience

• Let students role-play scenarios where manners are needed, such as: waiting in line, sharing an item such as glue or lunchtime.

Physical/Sensory Experience

• Mothers teach us to use good manners. See if your students remember to say, "Mother, May I?" when playing the old favorite game.

Arts/Crafts Experience

• Have students trace around key patterns, cut them out and make a pipe cleaner ring full of keys. Each key should be labeled with good manner words or phrases: *Thank You, Please, May I? I'm Sorry* and *You're Welcome.* See key patterns on page 152.

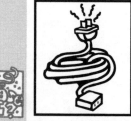

Extension Activities

• Invite students to an etiquette luncheon where they can practice good manners.

Values Education Experience

• Reinforce the value of courtesy in making and keeping friends.

Follow-Up/Homework Idea

• Encourage students to go home and practice good manners with their families.

150

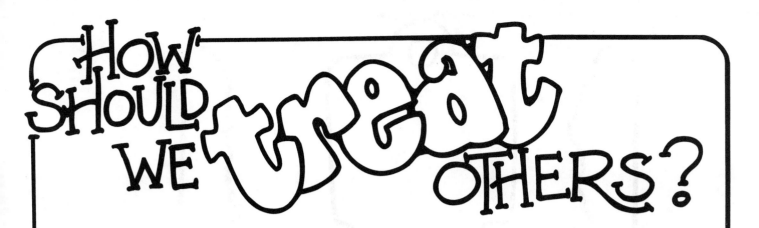

HOW SHOULD WE treat OTHERS?

Name: _____

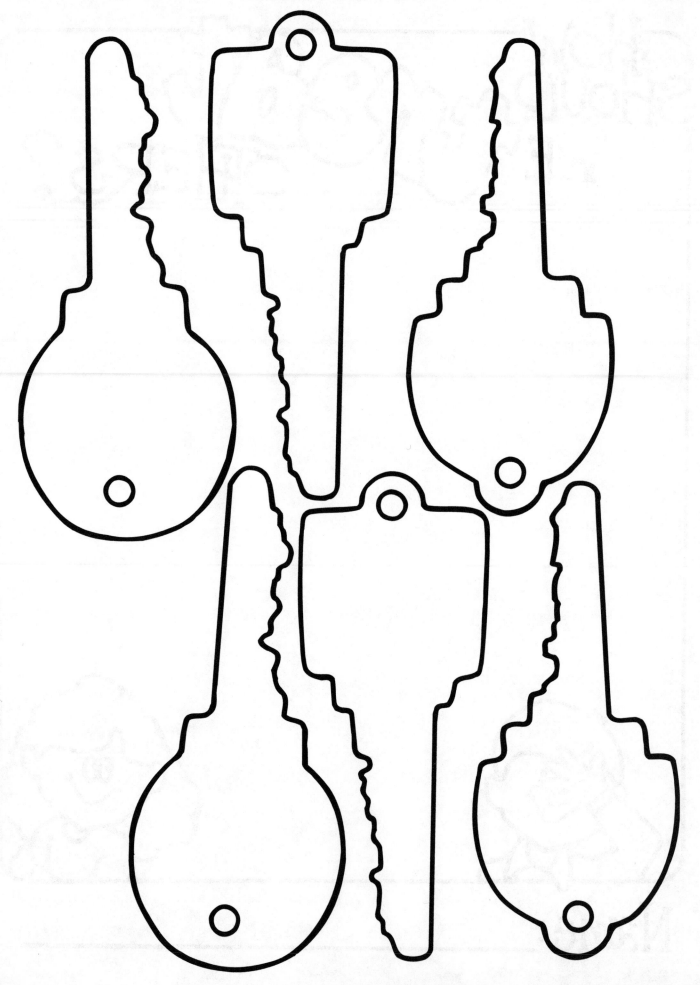

152

Feeling Feelings Day

August 25

Setting the Stage

- Display pictures of people showing different kinds of feelings around related literature.

- Construct a semantic web with what your students already know about feelings. Then list other things they want to be able to understand about expressing feelings.

Literary Exploration

Arnie and the New Kid by Nancy Carlson
Badger's Parting Gifts by Susan Varley
A Big Fat Enormous Lie by Marjorie Weinman Sharmat
Every Kid's Guide to Handling Feelings by Joy Berry
Feelings by Aliki
Feelings by Sue Clarke
Feelings by Joanne Murphy
Feelings Alphabet by Judy Lalli
Goodbye House by Frank Asch
I Have Feelings by Terry Berger
I Was So Mad! by Norma Simon
Lost! by David McPhail
Oliver Button Is a Sissy by Tomie dePaola
Sheila Rae, the Brave by Kevin Henkes
Temper Tantrum Book by Edna Preston
The Way I Feel . . . Sometimes by Beatrice Schenk De Regniers
What Feels Best? by Anita Harper
William's Doll by Charlotte Zolotow

Language Experience

- Let students brainstorm as many words that rhyme with the *feel*.

Feeling
Feelings

Feeling
Feelings

Feeling
Feelings

Writing Experience

• Have students write about one of the following story starters: See reproducible on page 157.

Sometimes I feel afraid when . . .
When I see people angry, I feel . . .
One time I was really scared when . . .
It always makes me feel good when . . .
I was so happy when . . .
I feel silly when . . .
I feel kind of sad when . . .
The times I feel the happiest are when . . .
I feel bad when . . .
After I've finished crying, I . . .
I think I would be happier if . . .
Sometimes I feel like crying when . . .
I feel important inside when . . .
The biggest fear I have is . . .
One time I got really mad when . . .
When I feel lonely inside, I . . .
I get embarrassed when . . .
My family shows their feelings at home by . . .

Name:

Science/Health Experience

- Today is a great day to begin a unit on all the different feelings a person can have and how to deal with them positively. Read aloud Joy Berry's *Every Kid's Guide to Handling Feelings* (ages 9-12) or Aliki's *Feelings* (ages 4-8).

Music/Dramatic Experience

- Let students role-play various emotional situations to practice dealing positively with their feelings. Using puppets may help them loosen up faster.

- Borrow (from a local library) Hap Palmer's sound recording of "Ideas, Thoughts and Feelings."

Physical/Sensory Experience

- Construct a Feeling-O-Meter from an empty tissue box and three paper towel tubes. On one tube draw several eye brow expressions (surprised, happy and angry). On a second tube draw eyes, and on the third tube draw mouths showing sad, mad and happy expressions. Students can use the Feeling-O-Meter, when they have a hard time expressing their feelings. They simply turn the tubes to the appropriate expressions. This can open the communication process.

Arts/Crafts Experience
• Let students make a collage from magazine picture cutouts of people exhibiting various emotions.

Values Education Experience
• Reinforce the value and importance of expressing one's feelings positively rather than keeping them bottled up.

Follow-Up/Homework Idea
• Encourage students to be good examples to their families by expressing their feelings in a constructive manner.

Feeling Feelings

Name: _____

Boat Bonanza Day

August 26

Setting the Stage

• Display student work samples around a picture of a boat with the caption: "We're Setting Sail for a Great New School Year!" or "Shipshape Work!"

• Construct a semantic web with facts your students already know (or would like to know) about boats and ships to help you structure the day's activities.

Literary Exploration

Baby's Boat by Jeanne Titherington
The Boat by Felix Monique
Boat Book by Gail Gibbons
Boat Ride with Lillian Two Blossom by Patricia Blaco
The Daddies Boat by Lucia Monfried
If I Sailed a Boat by Miriam Young
Little Boat by Michel Gay
The Little Boat by Kathy Henderson
Little Sail Boat by Lois Lenski
Lobster Boat by Brenda Guiberson
Louise Builds a Boat by Louise Pfanner
Mr. Gumpy's Outing by John Burningham
My Blue Boat by Chris Demarest
Nicole's Boat by Allen Morgan
Row, Row, Row Your Boat by Joanne Oppenheim
Sailing Ships by Ron Van derMeer
Song of the Boats by Lorenz Graham
Time of Wonder by Robert McCloskey
The Voyage of the Jolly Boat by Margret Rettich
Who Sank the Boat? by Patricia Allen
The Wreck of the Zephyr by Chris Van Allsburg

TLC10452 Copyright © Teaching & Learning Company, Carthage, IL 62321-0

Language Experience

• Review other words with the "oa" sound as in *boat*.

Writing Experience

• Let students imagine that they can set sail for anywhere in the world. Ask them to write about where they want to go and why. See reproducible on page 162.

If I could sail anywhere, where would I go?

Boat Captain's Name: _____

Science/Health Experience

• Learn how ships and boats are able to move and be steered across water in a definite path.

Social Studies Experience

• Study the history of boats and ships and where they have gone.

• Read *If You Sailed on the Mayflower in 1620* by Ann McGovern, for a lively look at life on board.

Music/Dramatic Experience
• Sing "Row, Row, Row Your Boat" as a round.

Physical/Sensory Experience
• Let students make old-fashioned sailboats from newspapers. Sail them in a sink or large tub.

• Purchase inexpensive model ships from hobby stores for students to put together.

Arts/Crafts Experience

- Have students paint pictures of a lake with a sunset of a gradation of warm colors (yellow, orange, red). Use graduating cool colors (blue, green, purple) for the water. While these are drying, have them cut out silhouettes of a sailboat from black construction paper. When they glue it over the lake picture they will have a beautiful contrasting scene. For a variation, students can tear strips of cool colors of construction paper for the lake, then slip the boat silhouette between the waves.

- Students can make sailboats from a walnut half (or a lunch milk carton bottom) by sticking a small dab of clay in the bottom and sticking a paper sail on a toothpick mast in the clay.

Extension Activities

- Students will enjoy this edible boating scene! Make raspberry blue gelatin. When it's set, stir it up to resemble blue waves. Make cheese slice triangle "sails" on toothpicks stuck into apple wedge sailboats. Place the sailboats in the gelatin waves.

Boat Captain's Name: _____

Mother Teresa's Birthday

August 27

Mother
Teresa

Mother
Teresa

Mother
Teresa

Setting the Stage

- Display pictures of people showing acts of kindness around related literature to focus interest.

Historical Background

The great humanitarian, Mother Teresa was born on this day in 1910, in Albania. Mother Teresa became a missionary nun, devoting her life to caring for the needs and suffering of others. She received the Nobel Peace Prize for her efforts to make this world a better place.

Literary Exploration

Mother Teresa by Joan Clucas
Mother Teresa by Mary Craig
Mother Teresa by Vanora Leigh
Mother Teresa by Mildred Pond
Mother Teresa by Richard Tames
Mother Teresa by Jill C. Wheeler
Mother Teresa: Friend to the Friendless by Carol Greene
Mother Teresa: Helping the Poor by William Jay Jacobs
Mother Teresa: Her Mission to Serve God by Charlotte Gray
Mother Teresa: Protector of the Sick by Linda Johnson
Mother Teresa: Sister to the Poor by Patricia Reilly Giff
Mother Teresa: The Early Years by David Porter

Language Experience

• How many synonyms can your students think of for the word *kindness*?

Writing Experience

• Have students write about what they would like to do to make the world a better place. See reproducible on page 167.

How I can make the world a better place.

Name: _____

• Students can make coupons for family members, neighbors or class members to redeem upon request. Examples: taking out an elderly neighbor's trash or pulling weeds for a busy single parent and so on. See patterns for Caring Coupons on page 168.

CARING COUPON

To: Dona Mae
From: Lewie
Good for: weeding in the garden

truck wash

Math Experience

- Set up math buddies today (those who catch on quicker with those who may need help). Let the buddies work together as you monitor their cooperative effort and accuracy.

Science/Health Experience

- Study the health-relief efforts instituted by Mother Teresa to help the sick, particularly in Calcutta, India.

Social Studies Experience

- Share biographical information of Mother Teresa. Learn how her organization, the Missionaries of Charity, provide medical care, food and housing for the needy in many, many countries around the world.

Arts/Crafts Experience

- Have students fold a piece of art paper in half. On one side have them illustrate Mother Teresa's efforts in kindness. On the other half, have them show their own efforts at being kind.

Extension Activities

- Decide on a class project: collecting donations for a homeless shelte visiting a nursing home or orphanage and so on. Let students get involved to gain an increased awareness and sensitivity to the needs others and, perhaps, a desire to help meet those needs.

Values Education Experience

- Today is a perfect opportunity to reflect upon the value of kindness and of serving others.

Follow-Up/Homework Idea

- Encourage students to make the world a better place, starting with acts of kindness right in their own homes.

How I can make the world a better place.

Name: _____

Caring Coupon

To: _____

From: _____

Good for: _____

Caring Coupon

To: _____

From: _____

Good for: _____

Caring Coupon

To: _____

From: _____

Good for: _____

Down on the Farm Day

August 28

On the
Farm

On the
Farm

On the
Farm

Setting the Stage

• Wear overalls and a straw hat, and stick a thin piece of hay or wheat in your pocket. Make your classroom look like a barn with a little bit of imagination and a few props.

• Display items and pictures of farm life around related literature to get students excited about the day.

Literary Exploration

Animals on the Farm by Feodor Rojankovsky
Animals Should Definitely Not Act Like People by Judi Barrett
The Baby Animals Party by Katharine Ross
Cock-A-Doodle Dudley by Bill Peet
Cock-A-Doodle-Doo by Franz Brandenberg
Cock-A-Doodle-Doo by Venice Shone
Color Farm by Lois Ehlert
Dumb Clucks! Jokes About Chickens by Rick Walton
Family Farm by Thomas Locker
The Farm Alphabet Book by Jane Miller
Farm Animals by Martin Andrews
Farm Animals by Ib Penick
Farm Book by Charles Roth
The Farm Booth by Elmer Boyd Smith
Farm Boy's Year by David McPhail
The Farm Counting Book by Jane Miller
Farm Day by Claire Henley
Farm Morning by David McPhail
Farm Noises by Jane Miller
The Farmer by Rosalind Kightley
Farmer Schulz's Ducks by Colin Thiele
Fiddle I Fee by Melissa Sweet
The Fine Family Farm by Stephen Cosgrove
Friendly Farm Animals by Esther K. Meeks
How Many Babies on the Farm? by Robert Crowther
Let's Look at All the Animals on the Farm by Harold Roth

Literary Exploration continued

Little Chicken by Margaret Wise Brown
Little Farm by Lois Lenski
My Day on the Farm by Chiyoke Nakatani
Night, Farm by Giora Carmi
Oh What a Noisy Farm by Harriett Ziefert
Old MacDonald Had a Farm by Carol Jones
Old MacDonald Had a Farm by Tracey Pearson
Old MacDonald Had a Farm by Glen Rounds
Once Upon Mac's Farm by Stephen Gammell
Our Animal Friends at Maple Hill Farm by Alice Provensen
Six Sick Sheep by Joanna Cole, et al.
A Visit to the Farm by Coby Hol
What's Inside? Small Animals by Dorling Kindersley

Language Experience

- Let students brainstorm other vowel controlled r's (ar, er, ir, or and ur) similar to the one in the word *barn*.

Writing Experience

• Have students write about a day on the farm from a farm animal's point of view. See reproducible on page 175.

My day on the farm...

Name: _____

Math Experience

• Provide students with animal crackers to use as math manipulatives to practice counting, addition and subtraction.

Science/Health Experience

- Today is a great day to begin a science unit on the farm and farm animals.

- Discuss products made or obtained from farm animals: eggs from hens, wool from sheep and so on.

Social Studies Experience

- Have children create a time line of events that follows an agricultural product from farm to consumer (for example: wool, popcorn, orange juice, peanut butter, etc.).

Music/Dramatic Experience

- Sing the traditional favorites, "Old MacDonald" and "The Farmer in the Dell."

- Let budding comedians tell a few jokes from the book, *Dumb Clucks! Jokes About Chickens* by Rick Walton.

172

Physical/Sensory Experience

- Let students play Farm Animal Charades! They can pantomime various farm animals for others to guess.

Arts/Crafts Experience

- Students will enjoy working together on a mural of a farm or a shoe box diorama with stand-up farm animals inside.

- Provide students with construction paper, felt scraps, wiggly eyes and pom-poms and have them make farm animal faces on paper sacks.

Extension Activities

• Visit a nearby farm to find out what a farmer does and how he cares for the animals.

• Invite a local farmer to visit your class and talk about the work of main taining the farm and caring for the animals.

• Would your students like to eat what farm animals eat? Serve them snacks such as seeds, nuts, fruit, corn and raw vegetables.

Follow-Up/Homework Idea

• Ask students to take an inventory of items found in their homes that originated on a farm: eggs, meat, cooking oil, wool, soy-based ink in newspapers, cotton balls, etc.

My day on the farm...

Name: _____

What's Cookin'? Day

August 29

Setting the Stage
• Display fascinating facts about your current study with cooking utensils or a picture of a chef with the caption: "What's Cooking?" or "Here's What's Cooking!"

Literary Exploration
Baking Like Mommy (Pillsbury Company)
Boston Cooking School Cook Book by Fannie Farmer
Dishes Children Love (Family Weekly Books)
Easy Cooking by Ann Beebe
In the Night Kitchen by Maurice Sendak
The Junior Baking Book (General Mills)
Let's Cook Without Cooking by Esther Rudomin
The Little Pigs' First Cookbook by N. Cameron Watson
My First Cookbook by Rena Coyle
Yummers by James Marshall

176

Language Experience

• Have students write an Edible Alphabet with each letter standing for something that can be eaten: A—asparagus, B—banana, C—cantaloupe and so on.

Writing Experience

• Let students write recipes for being a good student. Example: Mix 1 cup of hard work with 3 tablespoons of respect and ¼ cup of good listening.

• Ask students to imagine what is in the refrigerator at home (mystery leftovers and all). Have them write recipes using these items or imagine that the leftovers take on personalities of their own and take control of the other foods in the refrigerator. Encourage students to be creative. Let them share their papers with the class. See reproducible on page 181.

• Let each student write a favorite recipe. Compile all the recipes into a class cookbook.

Math Experience

- Involve students in measurement and estimation as they make the recipes the class chooses.

Science/Health Experience

- Review sanitation and cleanliness while working with food.

- Review safety procedures when working with utensils such as sharp knives and with electrical equipment, hot burners and ovens.

Social Studies Experience

- Study the history of cookbooks. Before the nineteenth century, recipe called for a "pinch of this and a handful of that." Fannie Farmer is credited with authoring the first cookbook with standard uniform measurements.

Music/Dramatic Experience

- Get students involved in cooperative group cooking! Divide them into pairs. Have one partner explain to the other how to make a certain recipe. Words only. No gestures. (Choose something easy such as making a sandwich.) The first partner must follow the other's directions. Let them switch roles so they can experience both roles. Reinforce the need for clear, concise instructions to avoid disasters.

Physical/Sensory Experience

- Browse through children's cookbook recipes to choose ones your students will want to try.

Fruit Salad

1 c. Mandarin Oranges
1 c. Seedless Grapes
1 c. Strawberries
2 Sliced Bananas
1 c. Whipped Topping

Combine all in a bowl and mix well.

No~Bake Cookies

1/4 c. Margarine
1 1/2 c. Sugar
1/3 c. Peanut Butter
1/2 c. Milk
3 T. Cocoa

Spoon by tablespoons onto wax paper and chill.

Combine in a saucepan and bring to a full boil and add:
3 c. Quick Oats
1 t. Vanilla

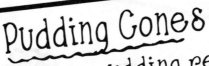

Pudding Cones

Prepare pudding recipe according to directions. Add 1 cup of whipped topping and chill. Spoon into ice cream cones and top with additional whipped topping and nuts or candies.

Arts/Crafts Experience
• Let students become food artists! Give them a variety of finger-type foods in different colors, smells and textures. Let them use their imaginations to make a person, place, thing or design from the food pieces.

Extension Activities
• Invite a local chef to visit your class and talk about preparing food.

Follow-Up/Homework Idea
• Challenge students to help their moms in the kitchen tonight!

180

Shapes and Sizes Day

August 30

Setting the Stage

• Display shapes in a variety of sizes around related literature to focus attention on shapes and sizes.

Literary Exploration

All About Shapes by Ruth Thomson
All Shapes and Sizes by Shirley Hughes
Flat Stanley by Jeff Brown
Fun with Sizes and Shapes by Jacqueline Buddle
If You Look Around You by Fulvio Testa
Is It Larger? Is It Smaller? by Tana Hoban
Look Around! by Leonaro Fisher
My Very First Book of Shapes by Eric Carle
Shapes by Rosalina Kightley
Shapes by Jan Pienkowski
Shapes by George Siede
Shapes by Gwenda Turner
Shapes to Show by Karen Gundersheimer
Shapes, Shapes, Shapes by Tana Hoban
Sizes by Jan Pienkowski
There's a Square: A Book About Shapes by Mary Serfozo

Language Experience

• Let students brainstorm as many shapes as they can think of: trapezoid, rhombus, circle, triangle, rectangle, square, hexagon. Then have them list the shapes in alphabetical order.

Math Experience

• Today is a perfect day to begin a unit on fractions or geometry!

Social Studies Experience

• Reinforce environmental reading with road signs of various shapes: stop sign, railroad sign, yield sign and so on.

Music/Dramatic Experience

• Play a game of 20 Questions with shapes! ("I'm thinking of an object in the room that is a triangle shape.")

Physical/Sensory Experience

- Have students use bendable drinking straws and pipe cleaners to mak as many different kinds of shapes as they can.

- Go on a neighborhood Shape Hunt! Walk around the school while students make observational drawings of all the shapes they see. Bac in the classroom, let them share their findings with the rest of the class.

- Today is a great day to play with hoola hoops!

Arts/Crafts Experience

- Take time today to let students create their own tessellations!

- Have students create pictures with hidden shapes then trade with friends and look for them. Or let a student draw a shape, then give it to classmates to turn it into something interesting.

- Cut sponges into different shapes and let students dip them into sponge paint of various colors to create a collage of shapes.

- Students will enjoy creating interesting shapes from clay.

Extension Activities

- Serve Edible Shapes, crackers that are circles, squares, hexagons, trian gles and so on. Have the students name the shapes as they eat them Younger students can match each cracker to the correct shape on their papers.

Follow-Up/Homework Idea

- Challenge students to count the different shapes they observe on the way home.

Summer Travels Day

August 31

Setting the Stage

- It's that time of year! Summer's winding down, soon days will be getting cooler. Today is a day to celebrate our memories of the summer, then pack them away with our seashells and postcards.

- Invite students to bring postcards and pictures of the places they visited over the summer. Display these around related literature.

- Construct a semantic web with words your students think of when you say, *summer vacation*.

Literary Exploration

Anno's USA by Mitsumasa Anno
How I Spent My Summer Vacation by Mark Teague
My Summer Vacation by Sumiko
On Vacation by Richard Scarry
Stringbean's Trip to Shining Sea by Vera B. Williams
What Ernie and Bert Did on Their Summer Vacation by Patricia Thackray

Summer
Travels

Summer
Travels

Summer
Travels

Language Experience

- Have each student write a short skit about a favorite book he or she read over the summer. Invite other classmates to participate in acting out the skit.

Writing Experience

- Let students write postcards from places they visited (or wanted to visi this past summer. They should write a message on the back of the postcard and draw a picture on the front. Remind them to write some where on the card, "Wish you were here!" See postcard patterns on page 190.

- It's tradition! Every teacher in grade school has students write about what they did during summer vacation. Here's your chance! See reproducible on page 191.

- Let students write letters to their teachers from last year to tell them about their summer.

186

Math Experience

• Let students survey schoolmates to find the favorite local vacation spot. Add the results to a class bar graph.

Social Studies Experience

• Have students bring postcards and pictures from various places they visited over the summer. Place these near a map and string a piece of yarn from each one to the correct place on the map.

Music/Dramatic Experience

• Divide students into cooperative groups to create raps, jingles or poems to sing or recite. The topic is "Good-Bye Summer" or "Ode to a Great Summer."

Physical/Sensory Experience

• Play Summer Vacation Relay! Divide the class into two teams. Give each team leader a suitcase full of large clothes and accessories. Players take turns opening the suitcase, putting on the vacation clothe (over their clothes) and "traveling" to a pre-determined "destination." Then he or she takes off the vacation clothes, puts them back in the suitcase, "travels" back "home" and gives it to the next person on the team. The team who has all their players "home" from vacation and sitting down, wins!

Arts/Crafts Experience

• Let students paint or draw favorite summer memories with pastel chalk

• Students can cut pictures from magazines to make a summer collage. It can be titled "Summer (year)" or placed in a suitcase-looking frame.

188

Values Education Experience

• Discuss the value in taking breaks between intense study or work to replenish and refuel before beginning again.

Follow-Up/Homework Idea

• Encourage students to work on summer scrapbooks with their families to preserve wonderful summer memories.

MY SUMMER VACATION!

Name: _____

192